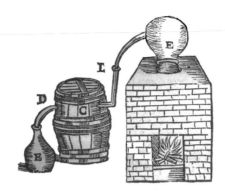

THE WHISKEYS OF IRELAND

'Aqua Vitae sloeth age, it strengtheneth youth, it helpeth digestion,

it cutteth flegme, it abandoneth melancholy,

it relisheth the hart, it lighteneth the mind,

it quickeneth the spirites.

Truly it is a soveraigne liquor,

if it be orderly taken.'

Richard Stanihurst (1577-1618)
Dubliner and alchemist to Philip II of Spain

'Whiskey, Irish for droplets of pure pleasure.'

WB Yeats

WITH THANKS TO:

I know exactly when the idea for this book started. I was bobbing around the Aegean with Oz Clark and a film crew; we were drinking bad wine and talking about good whiskey. That was a long time ago; my once skinny address book is now bulging with the names of people who helped me put this book together.

From the start, The O'Brien Press was a dream to work with. Michael O'Brien and Íde Ní Laoghaire believed in the project, and I had the pleasure of working with Eoin O'Brien and Emma Byrne, who did wonders with my half-crazed ravings and dodgy photos.

Within the industry, my thanks go to all in Bow Street, including Dr Barry Walsh, Dr Kevin MacNamara, Eily Kilgannon, Adrian Keogh and the incredibly hard-working Deirdre Farrell. At Midleton I am much in debt to Barry Crockett and Brendan Monks, and to Richard Burrows in Paris for taking my calls.

In County Antrim, my gratitude goes to Dave Quinn and Cliodhna Purcell; at the North Mall, to Sean O'Mahony and his team. Also many thanks to John Clement Ryan.

At Cooley I met a great bunch of people, including David Hynes, Noel Sweeney and John Harte. Big thanks also to Dr John Teeling for taking time out to talk to me; at Kilbeggan, thanks go to the always welcoming Bernadette and Brian Quinn.

I would also like to express my gratitude to Kevin Abrook at C&C International, David Phelan of Roaringwater Bay, Jonathan Mitchell at Mitchell & Son, Mark Andrews at Knappogue Castle, Tom Goff at Caffgo, Ives Tricoit at Hennessy, Tom Murphy at Knockeen Hills, Oliver Dillon at Bunratty, David Kilfoile at Shaw-Ross, Andrew Symington at Signatory and Jamie Walker at Adelphi.

On the research front, many thanks to Christine Jones at UDV, Eithlin Roche at the Guinness Archives, Michael Byrne at Offaly Historical Society, and local historians Ivor Doherty in Derry and Paddy Connolly in Bandon. Also the staff in the Boole library, UCC, and Magee University, Derry.

Big thanks to my Yahoo! Irish whiskey pals, Saint Roger of Danbury and Dr Alex R Kraaijeveld. Huge thanks to the amazing Gil Vernon, who brought his considerable editing skills to bear on my first drafts – I owe you one there in Wisconsin.

In Cork, at Dominic Moore's fire proved to be a great place to sip a ball of malt, while in Dublin Mum, Dad, Niamh, Paul, Aoife and Ciara were as supportive as ever. Finally, a huge 'thank you' goes to my beautiful wife Ruth and the amazing Tadhg Mulryan; they left me to get on with it, even though it took about a year longer than I said it would. Writers ...

The WHISKEYS of IRELAND

Peter Mulryan

THE O'BRIEN PRESS
DUBLIN

First published 2002 by
The O'Brien Press Ltd,
20 Victoria Road,
Dublin 6,
Ireland.
Tel: +353 1 4923333; Fax: +353 1 4922777
E-mail: books@obrien.ie
Website: www.obrien.ie

ISBN: 0-86278-751-3

British Library Cataloguing-in-Publication Data
Mulryan, Peter
The Whiskeys of Ireland
1.Whiskey - Ireland 2.Whiskey - Ireland - History 3.Whiskey industry -
Ireland - History
I.Title
641.2'52'09415

1 2 3 4 5 6 7 8 9 10
02 03 04 05 06 07 08

The O'Brien Press receives
assistance from

The Arts Council
An Chomhairle Ealaíon

Editing, layout and design: The O'Brien Press Ltd
Colour separations: C&A Print Services Ltd
Printing: Zure S.A.

Picture credits: Peter Mulryan: back cover, pp. 6, 8–9, 12–13, 17 (top), 19, 22 (both), 26, 29, 35, 36, 37, 40–41, 42–43, 46
(top), 49, 54 (top), 58, 59, 63 (top), 74, 75 (top), 77, 79, 82, 83, 84, 88–89, 91, 92, 95, 97, 98, 100 (all), 101, 102, 103 (both),
105, 107, 108, 111, 112, 113, 114, 115, 116, 118, 124–125; Irish Distillers Group: front cover, pp. 3, 28, 30–31, 38, 44–45, 47
(top), 48, 52–53, 56–57, 60, 61, 64–65, 66, 69, 70–71, 75 (bottom), 80, 81, 86–87, 90, 93, 96, 119, 122–123; Cooley Whiskey
PLC: pp. 21, 51, 85, 99; Petra Carter: p.119; Irish Arms: p.16; Guinness Ireland: p.20; National Museum of Ireland: p.25; United
Distillers and Vintners: pp. 39, 46 (bottom), 47 (bottom), 50; Comdt. E Kelly (via Military Archives): p.55; Paddy Connolly:
p.63 (bottom); Foynes Flying Boat Museum: p.68; Offaly Historical Society: pp. 72–73; Irish Examiner Publications: p.76;
Pepe's Bodega, Jerez: p.110.
Labels courtesy of Irish Distillers, Cooley PLC, C&C International and Davoc Rynne at www.Irelandcountryantiques.com.
Every effort has been made to contact the copyright holders for all pictures. If any omission or oversight has occured we
would request the copyright holder(s) to inform the publisher.

CONTENTS

Note on the spelling of 'whisk(e)y'

Nowadays all Irish whiskey is spelt with an 'e'. The last Irish whisky (without the 'e') was Paddy, produced by the Cork Distilleries Company prior to the formation of Irish Distillers in 1966.

Throughout this book, whiskey is spelt with an 'e' unless I am referring to Scotch whisky, or quoting somebody or some product title with no 'e' in it.

It is amazing how many pub arguments revolve around this topic. However, the spelling of the word is really of little importance, as it is simply a corruption of the Gaelic word *uisce*, meaning 'water'.

INTRODUCTION

'When I drink whiskey, I drink whiskey, and when I drink water, I drink water.'
Barry FitzGerald, The Quiet Man *(1952)*

One crisp afternoon in December, eighty years after spirit last flowed from the stills, I found myself walking through the corpse of Cassidy's Distillery in Monasterevin, County Kildare. The famous 'beehive' domed mash house still stands and, behind the rumble of Cork-bound traffic, a spur of the River Barrow can still be heard running beneath the crumbling stonework.

In the still house, a single tree reaches for the low winter light leaking through the broken roof. The pot stills are long gone, though the curved redbrick recess that once held them, and the fire grates beneath, remain. This is a sad place, full of creeping ivy and doors going nowhere.

There is something strangely emotional about distilleries, especially long-dead ones. Maybe it is because each is as individual as we are, possessing a unique spirit that, once lost, can never be replaced. Maybe it is just because Ireland has lost so many.

Over the previous year, I visited all three of Ireland's working distilleries, and I also made a pilgrimage to at least another twenty sites that, in the late Victorian era, produced the known world's whiskey of choice – Irish pot still whiskey.

This is a journey few have undertaken. It took me from happy places like Bushmills in the far north of the country, and the prosperous town of Midleton in the far south, to distillery graveyards like Tullamore in the midlands, Phoenix Park in Dublin and Galway in the west; from the new distillery on the Cooley peninsula in County Louth, to the ancient one in Kilbeggan, County Westmeath.

The Irish whiskey industry has always reflected the nation as a whole. The granting of the first 'patents' to distil signalled the arrival of English law, and then came the famine years, the Victorian boom, the struggle for independence, and the hard years of economic war, depression and recession. More recently, Ireland's 'Celtic Tiger' economy signalled rebirth, with the arrival of Pernod Ricard's global outlook and the new Cooley Distillery.

In this book, alongside household names like Jameson, you will find tasting notes for over fifty other representations of Irish whiskey, many of which didn't exist ten years ago. Some, like Powers and Tullamore Dew, might ring a bell; others, like Inishowen and Hewitt's, will be new to most people. So, no matter what your level of knowledge, welcome to the adventure! Use this book as you would a road map and remember, there are no rules, except for one important one: Never water another man's whiskey.

Go n-éirí an bóthar libh!
Peter Mulryan
Clonakilty, West Cork, March 2002

The facade of the Shamrock Bar, Dunmanway, County Cork. In common with many pubs all over rural Ireland, the front of the pub would have held a small grocery store, with the drink served in the public bar at the rear.

THE R

ISE AND FALL

WHISKEY FROM THE DAWN OF TIME
TO THE VICTORIAN BOOM

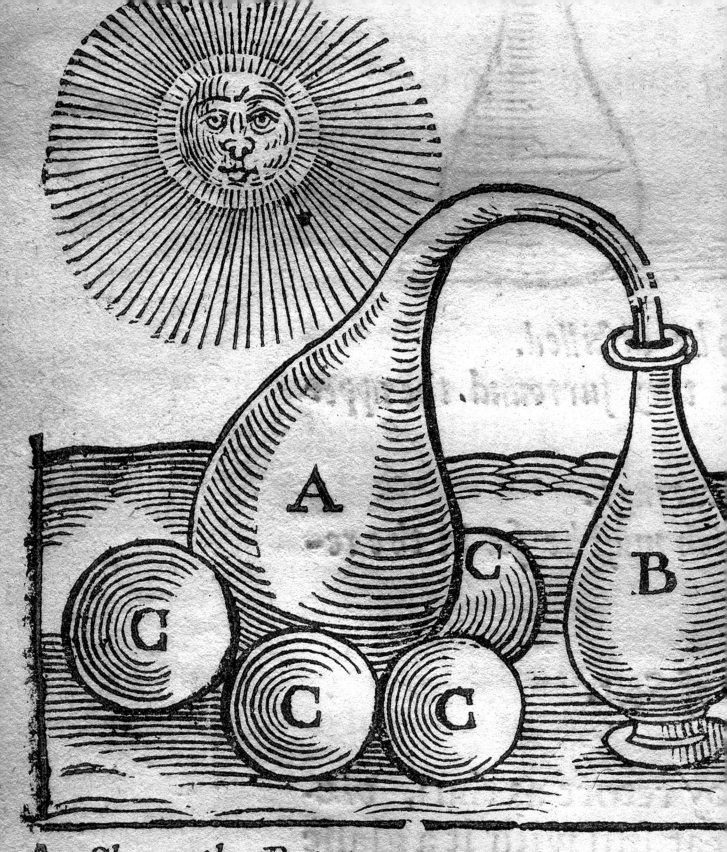

A, *Shews the Retort.*
B, *The Receiver.*
C, *The Cryſtall Bowles.*

1. MISTS OF TIME

'Aqua Vitae sloeth age, it strengtheneth youth,
it helpeth digestion, it cutteth flegme, it abandoneth melancholy,
it relisheth the hart, it lighteneth the mind, it quickeneth the spirites.
Truly it is a soveraigne liquor, if it be orderly taken.'

Richard Stanihurst (1577–1618), Dubliner and alchemist to Philip II of Spain

Once upon a time, Irish monks, or some would say Saint Patrick himself, invented an elixir, which was held in such reverence that it merited the name 'uisce beatha' – nothing less than the water of life itself.

The truth, while a lot less fanciful, is a lot more fascinating. For a start we know that the Irish didn't invent whiskey – but neither did the Scots. In all probability it was the Moors who discovered, or possibly even rediscovered, the art of distilling,

Pages 8–9: Autumn on the Dungourney River, County Cork. Since 1825, this river has provided the water for distilling in the town of Midleton. These pages: Although the wonderful imagery in John French's *Of the Art of Distillation*, published in 1651, is pure alchemy, his text marks a major move away from that philosophy. French was in fact a follower of the Paracelsian school of chemistry, one which was sceptical of alchemical traditions and more intent on seeking medical uses for chemical compounds like alcohol.

11

sometime in the eleventh century. Being Muslim, and therefore in theory teetotal, their still was used for medicinal rather than recreational purposes.

No one knows when the alembic was first set to produce alcohol, but we do know that in the thirteenth century Arnold de Villa Nova, a Moorish alchemist, distilled wine, producing a spirit his contemporaries called 'alcohol', a corruption of the Arabic *al-kohl*.

When the Moors were pushed out of Europe by the Catholic armies of Spain, the art of distilling fell into the hands of monks, who brought the knowledge to every corner of the known world. It would seem that the 'water of life' was almost universal, and just about any native plant could be pressed into service: in France, *eau-de-vie* was made from grapes; in Scandinavia *aquavit* from herbs; and in Ireland *uisce beatha* from grain.

The first widely quoted mention of 'whiskey' in relation to Ireland comes from the *Annals of the Four Masters*. It tells the story of the chieftain Risterd Mac Ragnaill, who, one evening in 1405, 'entered into rest after drinking usci bethad to excess, it was a deadly water to him.'

In all probability the drink being referred to is not whiskey, but yet another water of life, the Roman drink *aqua vitae*. This was made not from grain, but from wine or brandy, and was very common in Ireland at the time. Of course there is no way of being sure, but a 1450 statute mentions 'Irish wine, ale or other liquor ...' Whiskey is notable by its absence, so it cannot have been very widespread.

Tracing the early evolution of Irish whiskey is therefore very difficult. For a start, there is little in the way of written records, and the few documents that do exist rarely make it clear whether Roman *aqua vitae* (made from wine), or Irish *aqua vitae* (made from native grain), is in question. To add to the confusion, the Gaelic term *uisce beatha* could refer to either drink. In his journal of 1600, Fynes Moryson, secretary to the English Lord Deputy, praised the medicinal value of Irish 'aqua vitae, vulgarly called usquebaugh'.

The first clear and unambiguous reference to *aqua vitae* being distilled from cereal comes in 1494, and then it is not in Ireland, but in Scotland. The Scottish exchequer records: 'To Friar John Cor, by order of the King, to make aqua vitae, viii bolls of malt ...' In Scotland a boll was equal to six Imperial bushels and, as every schoolchild knows, an Imperial bushel is the best part of ten kilograms. So Friar John and the other Benedictine monks wouldn't have had much time for evensong, as they had their hands full with around 500 kilograms of malt, enough to make 400 modern bottles of Scotch.

If grain was being distilled in Scotland in 1494, it is pretty safe to assume that it was also being distilled in Ireland. But the Irish tradition was an oral one, so few contemporary records exist, and those that do are largely English. Crown law didn't mean much beyond the Pale, a large ditch encircling the Crown-controlled lands around Dublin, and most distilling happened away from the east coast, in poorer Gaelic Ireland.

By the time that 'graine in making of aqua vitae' is first documented in Ireland, distilling fever had clearly gripped the land. An Act passed in 1556 by the English parliament in Ireland declares that, 'aqua vitae a drink nothing profitable to be daily drunken and used is now universally through the realm of Ireland.' This piece of legislation went on to make it illegal for anybody, with the exception of peers, gentlemen and the freemen of the larger towns, to distil *aqua vitae* without a licence from the Lord Deputy.

But the power of the English crown didn't extend very far. Beyond the Pale lay the anarchy of Gaelic Ireland, a land of ancient Brehon laws and warring Gaelic chiefs, too busy fighting each other to worry much about the English.

We get an insight into this way of life in the story of Turloch Luineach O'Neill, the most powerful of the Gaelic

The sun rises over a seventeenth-century ruined castle near Cullahill in County Laois.

13

Below: Elizabeth I, the English monarch who successfully colonised Ireland.

chieftains, who was pronounced dead in 1583. Clan chiefs from every corner of the island descended on Tyrone in an attempt to win favour and be crowned the next 'O'Neill'. However, Turloch wasn't dead at all – he had merely drunk himself into a coma. When word of the man's prestigious drinking feat spread, his reputation was further enhanced – here was a man among men; a man truly fit to lead the Irish.

With opposition like this, it is no wonder that Queen Elizabeth I was able to steadily extend her influence in Ireland. However, thirteen years later, when Turloch's successor Hugh O'Neill took the throne, there was a seismic shift in Gaelic politics.

The Ulster armies of Hugh O'Neill, along with those of his son-in-law Hugh O'Donnell, slowly started to move south, pushing back Elizabeth's forces. By 1580, their power base greatly reduced, the English imposed martial law in the nominally loyal province of Munster. Among

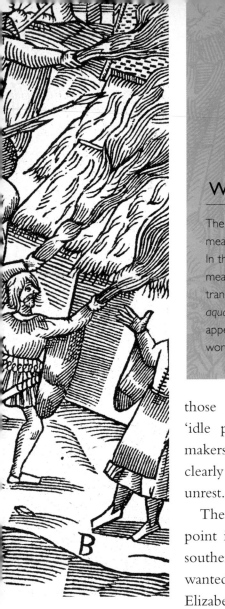

B

Water of life

The word 'whiskey' is a corruption of the Gaelic word *uisce*, meaning 'water'.

In the Gaelic languages of Ireland and Scotland, *uisce beatha* means 'the water of life'. This in itself is probably a direct translation of the Roman *aqua vitae* or the Scandinavian *aquavit*. Various spellings of *uisce*, such as '*uisge*' and '*usci*', appeared until the 1960s, when the spelling of Irish language words was standardised.

those who could be executed were 'idle persons ... aiders of rebels ... makers of aqua vitae ...' Spirits were clearly seen as one of the causes of unrest.

The situation in Ireland reached a crisis point in 1601, when a Spanish force landed in the southern port of Kinsale. This was the support O'Neill wanted. Even the Munster chiefs, previously loyal to Elizabeth, fell in behind the forces of Philip of Spain. The Catholic armies seemed invincible. From Kinsale they would sweep away all before them, secure Ireland and then move on London, deposing the heretic Elizabeth and placing a Catholic on the English throne. In the same way that his ancestors had driven the Moors from Europe, Philip of Spain would now sweep away Protestantism. The day before the Battle of Kinsale, Lord Mountjoy is reported to have despaired, 'The Kingdom is lost this day ...'

But, of course, the kingdom wasn't lost. If it had been, Ireland would now have its own royal family, for Philip was all set to put his daughter Isabella on the Irish throne, and this book would be written in Spanish. What did happen revolved around a bottle of whiskey.

According to legend, the Irish battle plans were betrayed to Lord Deputy Mountjoy in exchange for a bottle of *uisce beatha*. This could be nothing more than a contemporary myth, a fable to illustrate how even in their finest

Top left: The woodcuttings of John Derrick are basically a seventeenth-century newsreel, illustrating the English conquest of Ireland. In this plate, an armed company, carrying halberds and pikes, attack and burn a farmhouse and drive off the horses and cattle.
Above: King Philip II of Spain, at the time the most powerful ruler in the world.

Below: A replica of a seventeenth-century leather bottle and mugs, of the type used during the Battle of Kinsale.

hour, the Irish were beaten by their own vices. We will probably never know. What we do know is that the Gaelic troops had no experience of open battle. Out of communication with the Spanish, their formations were smashed by English cavalry and they were cut down in their thousands as they fled the battlefield. After a brief skirmish, the Spanish surrendered and Mountjoy and his men walked away with victory.

Following the defeat at Kinsale came the collapse of the Gaelic order. O'Neill, along with the other major Irish chieftains, fled to Europe, in what became known as the 'Flight of the Earls'. They planned to come back at the head of a massive invasion force, but there would never be another Spanish invasion, and they would never return.

With the departure of the native Irish leaders, the way was left open for the total colonisation of the island. It was the end of Gaelic Ireland, and all, perhaps, for a bottle of whiskey.

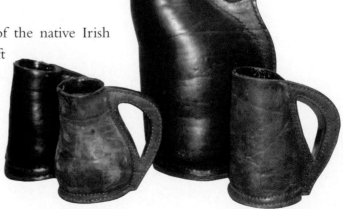

2. TAXING TIMES

The Dutchman for a drunkard
The Dane for golden locks
The Irishman for uisca beatha
The Frenchman for the pox

John Marston, Playwright, 1604

Above: The once thriving Locke's Distillery in Kilbeggan now houses a museum, while whiskey still matures in its ancient warehouses, which date from the mid-eighteenth century.

Whiskey and heritage seem to go hand in hand. In fact, it is hard to find a bottle of Irish that doesn't have some sort of date stamped on it, whether it is Jameson 1780 or Bushmills 1608. So, when Cooley Distillery set up shop in 1989, the first thing they did, way ahead of distilling anything, was to buy themselves some history. The old Locke's brand was given a dusting down, and Cooley now had a date to stick on their bottles – 1757.

What all of these brands have in common is a desperate craving to connect the stainless-steel reality of modern distilling with what Tullamore Dew promotional material refers to as 'days of golden glory'. But this mythical time only ever really existed in the minds of the people who market whiskey and in the cartoons of Walt Disney. It is all too easy to bring our rose-tinted, twenty-first-century sensibilities to bear on history. However, 400 years ago the world was a very different place.

For a start, people in Ireland either ate well or teetered on the brink of famine. It was a world of extremes, where the potato was still unknown and a favourite dish was jellied blood, eaten with salt and rancid butter. Carrion, horse and animal entrails were also enjoyed, as was ale brewed from bog myrtle and whiskey distilled from native grain.

At the start of the seventeenth century, as Crown law crept slowly and inexorably across the island, there was no whiskey industry. Everyone and anyone could distil; it was a cottage industry, and as much a part of everyday life as butter-making or weaving. It was a great way of using up surplus grain – whiskey didn't go off; it could be traded, rubbed on as a cure-all or taken internally for its 'medicinal' properties. Whiskey not only kept out the damp; it was used in the treatment of everything from cancer to the common cold. Drunk socially, it took people away from their miserable existences to a better place.

With the flight of the Irish earls to Europe in 1607, the Gaelic order and the native Brehon law collapsed, to be replaced by English nobility and English law. Things that used to be free, like distilling, were now controlled, and the first 'licences' governing distilling date from this time.

Patents

During Tudor times it was a common and corrupt practice for the English Crown to sell monopolies. These monopolies, or 'patents', were sold for just about anything – the importation of sweet wine, the brewing of beer or the distillation of whiskey for example. In return for either a cash payment or a proportion of the take (hence the term 'royalty'), the patent holder, usually a favourite of the court, was given a state guaranteed monopoly in a particular area, and could, in turn, sublet the licence for whatever fee they could extract.

The first Irish whiskey patent was granted by the Lord Deputy, Sir Arthur Chichester, to a Charles Waterhouse in Munster in January 1608, and subsequent patents were granted to Walter Taillor of County Galway and George Sexton of Leinster. By this time, the monopoly system was so rotten with cronyism and corruption that it was close to collapse. But this didn't stop the always-broke Chichester from granting his deputy for the occupation of Ulster, Sir Thomas Phillipps, a patent to distil in County Antrim on 20 April of the same year. It is from this 'grant of licence to make aquavitae' that the Old Bushmills Distillery claims its ancient heritage, although the distillery itself wasn't registered until 1784.

It was costing the Crown a fortune to keep an army in hostile Ireland, and the government finances were in a terrible mess. Things came to a head in 1641, when the state could not raise £50 to fight the Catholic uprising. The system would have to change. Monopolies were finally abolished and, on 24 December 1661, the king gave the Irish a special present: he taxed their Christmas toddy. It was the start of customs and excise as we know it today, and the result was the start of illegal distilling. From now on, Ireland would have two national drinks – 'parliament whiskey' and illegal *poitín*.

The law, however, was full of holes. Distillers didn't have to register, and the magistrates who were meant to enforce the law were often the local

Above: Irish Distillers claim that Old Bushmills is the oldest whiskey distillery in the world, dating from 1608. This is not strictly true. While a licence to distil was granted in that year, it was only registered as a legitimate distillery in 1784, and the buildings at the Old Bushmills Distillery date from the 1880s, making this the oldest working distillery in Ireland, but not the oldest in the world.

19

'Crowning its summit is a vast
cupola, surmounted by a brazen
figure of Ireland's patron saint,
mitre and crozier in hand.'

Alfred Barnard, 1887

landlords. They knew that many of their tenants relied on distilling to pay their rent. So, for exactly a century, corruption and self-interest were as rife as tax evasion.

Precisely when Ireland's first 'distillery' fired up its pot stills is therefore open to debate. Until 1761, registration was voluntary and entailed paying tax, so it will come as no surprise that prior to this there is little record of whiskey-making in Ireland. However, we do know, for example, that in 1757, when Matthew MacManus opened shop in Kilbeggan and Peter Roe started distilling in Thomas Street, Dublin, both gentlemen took over existing distilleries. John Locke eventually bought out the former, while, three generations down the line, the latter, George Roe and Son, would become Dublin's largest and most productive complex. But who owned the original plants, and when they were established, we will never know.

You wouldn't recognise the whiskey of times past as 'whiskey'. By modern standards, what passed the lips of our ancestors in 1780, 1757, or even 1608, was pretty foul stuff. The modern drink is mellowed by at least three years' maturation in oak casks; this spirit was drunk straight from the still, often flavoured with herbs in rather the same way that gin is today. When Dr Johnson came to visit Ireland in 1750, he found that, apart from it being 'particularly distinguished for its pleasant and mild flavour', Irish whiskey was a 'compounded, distilled spirit, being drawn on aromatiks'. This practice was widespread, for in Scotland it was recorded that 'distillation was from thyme, mint, anise and other fragrant herbs'.

By the middle of the eighteenth century, the demand for whiskey was such that quality control was less of a priority than production volume. In 1759 the standard of whiskey being produced in Ireland was so dismal and dangerous that parliament was forced to pass an Act prohibiting distillers from using any ingredient except malt, grain, potatoes and sugar. It specifically prohibited 'potash, lime, bog-gall or any other unwholesome or pernicious material or ingredient'.

It is hard to follow the early history of distilling in Ireland, as it was a time of great turmoil and rebellion. But nuggets of information like the above provide us with a wonderful window on a rapidly changing world, a world that was about to explode beyond all recognition.

Opposite: St Patrick's Windmill in the Liberties area of Dublin is now part of the Guinness complex. Its sails are long gone, but it once provided all the power for George Roe and Son, Ireland's largest pot still distillery. Below: John Locke III, grandson of the founder of Locke's Distillery.

Poitín (anglicised as Poteen, Potcheen, Potheen, etc.)

The word *poitín* is Irish for 'little pot' and is shortened from '*uisge poitín*'. Until 1661, *uisge beatha* and *uisge poitín* were one and the same, both being white spirits distilled from native grain, and for a time after this date the only difference between them was that duty was paid on *uisge beatha* and not on *uisge poitín*. As time marched on, the two drinks drifted farther apart. *Uisge beatha* embraced maturation and the marketplace, to become the Irish whiskey we all know and love. *Uisge poitín*, however, stayed in the primordial bogs of Ireland, shunning change and embracing infamy.

While molasses and Burco boilers have replaced barley and little black pots, little else has changed in the world of illegal *poitín*. It is still made in secret, on the damp mountainsides of Ireland, and enjoys a love-hate relationship with the law. In researching this book I asked a local journalist if he knew of any active *poitín* makers in his area. He suggested I contact the local Garda sergeant. Had there been a recent arrest, I asked? No, he replied, the sergeant was the *poitín* maker!

Given tales like this, which proved to be untrue, it is not surprising that *poitín* is inextricably bound up with the kind of romantic rogueism that marketing men would kill for. The Revenue authorities were not at all happy when Bunratty businessman Oliver Dillon announced in 1989 that he wanted to call a legal, duty-paid spirit '*poitín*'. However, an accommodation was finally reached, and today there are two legal brands of '*poitín*' on the market – the triple-distilled Knockeen Hills Poteen, produced in strengths up to 90% alcohol by volume (abv); and Bunratty Potcheen, single-distilled at 40% abv.

3. PARLIAMENT WHISKEY

'The manufacture of illicit spirits has long been a favourite beverage in Ireland, being made from malt without adulteration.'
Samuel Morewood, A Philosophical and Statistical History of the
Inventions and Customs of Ancient and Modern Nations in the
Manufacture of Inebriating Liqueurs *(1838)*

By 1760, the world was on the brink of the biggest change since man stopped foraging for food and started farming. A population boom, a growth in agricultural output and increased mechanisation were just some of the factors fuelling rapid change. The pursuit of money had replaced the mere struggle for survival. The English parliament, which by now was under the control of the merchant classes, fanned the flames of revolution.

Then, in 1769, Scotsman James Watt added a cooling chamber to a fifty-year-old invention called the steam engine, and the Industrial Revolution was born. Steam would change the world forever.

Above: A view across the portico of the parliament building in College Green, Dublin, from an eighteenth-century engraving by James Malton.

23

In Ireland, the Industrial Revolution never got much further than Belfast. The rest of the country remained a rural backwater, plagued by large families and ravaged by emigration. Landless, the average Irishman worked a small potato farm for a landlord who charged an exorbitant rent. Poverty was rampant and living conditions were appalling. Dublin, once the second city of the British Empire and the seventh largest in the world, was eclipsed as people fled the land to work in Liverpool, Manchester and Glasgow.

What limited industrialisation there was revolved around the country's biggest industry – agriculture. Distilling, which required nothing more than water, yeast and grain, was the perfect marriage of industry and agriculture. The early industrial distilleries of the time were small-time operations, and every town or village would have had a still, or possibly several, catering for a very local market.

Going Underground

Since 1661 distillers had been taxed on the volume of spirit that they sold, but in a country where the law was mostly a phantom, this proved very hard to police. For a hundred years, the law was most widely observed in its avoidance. In 1779 Lord North's London government decided to radically overhaul the excise. Since the size of all legal stills was known, the new plan was to tax the still, rather than its output. In theory this would make collecting tax easier and would guarantee the government a set income. When the law came into force there were 1,228 distilleries in Ireland; a year later there were a mere 246 registered with the State.

Where did they all go? Underground, of course. The system was unworkable – before distillers had even fired up a still they owed tax. In the rush for the hills, 'parliament whiskey' all but disappeared and *poitín* became the drink of the people.

Those few distilleries that stayed on the right side of the law had to battle for survival. The only way they could get ahead of the excise was to charge and recharge their stills more often than was permitted. With a fixed tax payable on the theoretical output of a still, distillers made their money by squeezing in as many extra distillations as they could. The heat was turned up so that the spirit would run off more quickly.

Opposite above: The boiler shop of Galloway & Sons, Manchester, in the heart of England's industrial belt. This type of large-scale manufacturing industry largely bypassed Ireland.
Opposite below: An illustration from an advert for Daniel Miller & Co., coppersmiths and brassfounders, Church Street, Dublin, close to the Jameson Distillery.
Below: Illegal distilling in Ireland was just a part of everyday life, as seen in this nineteenth-century photograph.

According to Aeneas Coffey, an excise officer in Donegal, the Inishowen peninsula had at least 800 illegal stills.

But violent evaporation led to excess frothing, and this in turn choked the worm and slowed things down. To get around the problem, soap was added to the mix. This kept the froth down, but now the whiskey tasted foul.

In a single month, the average licensed 300-gallon still went through nearly a ton of soap in this way. Not surprisingly, 'parliament whiskey' soon had a reputation as gut rot, while the illegal distiller producing *poitín* did so at his own pace and so made a superior product.

In 1783 the government decided that it had to do something to bolster the industry. Like most pieces of whiskey legislation, it backfired spectacularly. A £20 fine was imposed on any town where distilling apparatus was found. In poorer areas this caused real problems, as innocent communities were often punished for the crimes of others. Old scores were settled, as worn bits of equipment were planted to frame innocent people. Many lives were ruined.

By 1822 there were only forty legitimate distilleries operating in Ireland, and the following year there were just twenty. At the same time, according to Aeneas Coffey, an excise officer in Donegal, the Inishowen peninsula had at least 800 illegal stills. These were the *poitín* years. In some parts of the country it was sold as openly as bread, while in other areas moonshiners and excise men fought vicious running battles. During one of these clashes the aforementioned Coffey suffered a cracked skull and had a bayonet plunged twice through his thigh. However, he survived this encounter and went on to become Inspector General of Excise. Others weren't so lucky: another excise man, GE Howard, wrote that 'revenue officers are frequently assaulted, wounded and sometimes killed in the execution of their duty.'

Below: Theobald Wolfe Tone, who famously named England as 'the never failing source of all Ireland's ills'.

This was a time of revolution in North America and across Europe. Not to be outdone, in 1798 the United Irishmen, led by Theobald Wolfe Tone, rose in rebellion. Prime minister William Pitt took advantage of the unsuccessful revolt to introduce the 1800 Act of Union. Ireland's parliament (which had operated under the watchful eye of London anyway) voted itself out of existence, thus creating the United Kingdom of Great Britain and Ireland.

With Catholics denied representation in parliament, direct rule was a ticking time bomb. In 1805 the British government inadvertently lit the fuse when it introduced the Corn Laws. Designed to protect the business interests of the aristocratic landowners who peopled the House of Lords, these laws banned distillers from importing cheap foreign grain.

The world's largest pot still can be seen in the old Midleton Distillery, County Cork. Opposite: The statue of total abstinence campaigner Father Mathew in Patrick Street, Cork.

Within five short years, five million out of a population of just over eight million had taken 'the pledge'.

In 1823 the government swept away the old still tax; from now on, distillers would only pay duty on what they produced. The effect was drastic and immediate. In 1821 there were just thirty-two licensed whiskey makers in the land; by 1835 this number had mushroomed to ninety-three.

In 1823 the largest pot still in the country could hold only 750 gallons, yet two years later Midleton Distillery was boasting the world's largest pot still, with a capacity of 31,500 gallons. It was so large that it had to be assembled on-site, and the distillery building constructed around it.

In Bow Street, John Jameson, at the tender age of eighty-three, set £4,000 aside to update the plant. Unfortunately he died that very year, but his son (also John Jameson) put his plans into action.

Business was booming and Irish distilleries were expanding, pushing technology and embracing every modern innovation as their whiskeys conquered the world. 'The demand for Irish whiskey is practically unlimited at present,' said a Distillers Company Limited report from the late 1850s. Yet the country was spiralling into poverty. In 1833 a commission reported that nearly two-and-a-half million people were living in distress, and many were losing themselves in alcohol.

The spectres of emigration, poverty and alcoholism were tearing apart the fabric of Irish society. A response from Church and State was urgently needed. The 1838 Poor Law established the first Irish workhouses, while in that same year Father Theobald Mathew began his 'total abstinence' campaign.

Father Mathew, a charismatic and controversial Capuchin Friar from County Cork, led a remarkable crusade against 'the demon drink'. Within five short years, five million out of a population of just over eight million had taken 'the pledge', vowing total abstinence from the evils of alcohol. Almost overnight, twenty distilleries bit the dust, including Donegal's only ever legal operation. The industry had been dealt a blow from which it would never fully recover.

4. THE COFFEY REVOLUTION

*'The patent still people strip the spirit of all it ought to possess. As a man
stripped of his garments is still a man, although not fit in such a state to enter
into society, so the bare silent spirit is still spirit, but it is not fit for any of the
dietetic uses to which spirit may be beneficially applied.'*

Truths About Whisky, *1878*

Distilling in pot stills is a slow and messy business. The
whiskey is made in batches in copper pots that have to
be filled, heated, cooled, emptied and then filled again.
The spirit that has evaporated then passes to a second
set of stills and the process starts again. In the cases of
Bushmills and Midleton, where a system of triple-
distillation is in operation, this is repeated a third time. Nothing much has
changed over the centuries. Pot stills are, and have always been, expensive
and wasteful; indeed, it is their very inefficiency that helps to produce a high
quality, full-flavoured spirit.

In the nineteenth century, however, quality and flavour weren't always the

A view of the five pot stills in
Power's John's Lane Distillery,
c.1910. The building now
houses the National College
of Art and Design, where
some of the pot stills can
still be seen.

priorities. Much of the spirit produced wasn't drunk as whiskey, but was sent to Cork or to London to be rectified into gin. Alcohol also had many industrial uses, so the taste of the raw product was less important than its alcohol content. The more potent the liquor, the further it would go.

Across the Empire and beyond, the hunt was on for a more efficient way to distil. In 1830 the most important in a series of still design patents was lodged by none other than Aeneas Coffey, the former Inspector General of Excise in Ireland. Complete with bayonet wounds from the *poitín* wars, and in the greatest of ironies, Coffey had retired from the service to become a distiller. His arrival would change everything.

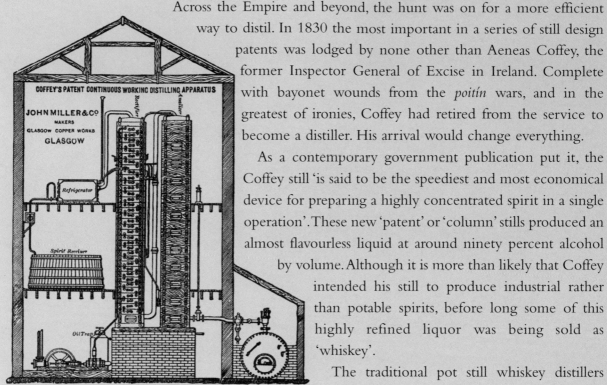

As a contemporary government publication put it, the Coffey still 'is said to be the speediest and most economical device for preparing a highly concentrated spirit in a single operation'. These new 'patent' or 'column' stills produced an almost flavourless liquid at around ninety percent alcohol by volume. Although it is more than likely that Coffey intended his still to produce industrial rather than potable spirits, before long some of this highly refined liquor was being sold as 'whiskey'.

The traditional pot still whiskey distillers derided patent still whiskey, calling it 'silent [i.e. tasteless] spirit'. However, contrary to popular folklore, the Irish did not shun this new innovation; in fact they embraced it. Within ten years of Coffey lodging his patent, there were thirteen of his stills operating in Ireland, compared with just two in Scotland. By 1900 the number of column stills was down to single figures, though they still accounted for over seventy percent of whiskey produced in Ireland.

From the start, the 'big four' Dublin firms of John Jameson, William Jameson, John Power and George Roe looked down their noses at both Aeneas and his invention. 'These things,' they declared of column stills, 'no more yield Whisky than they yield wine or beer.' The Dublin distillers were content in the knowledge that nothing could match the quality and the consistency of their full-flavoured pot still whiskey.

Meanwhile, the Irish economy was creaking to a halt, and Aeneas Coffey left the country for the more prosperous and welcoming Scottish and English markets. As he did, a bizarre sequence of events was beginning to unfold, which would ultimately catch the entire Irish whiskey industry with its pants down.

Above: 'Coffey's Patent Continuous Distilling Apparatus', as manufactured by John Miller & Co. of Glasgow. The highly potent spirit produced by the new invention was almost tasteless, and so could easily be flavoured to make cheap gin, brandy or even whiskey.

Blended Scotch

The Scots and the English had little to lose in adopting the Coffey still. Although they were expensive to install and operate, what they could produce in a week would take a whole nine-month season to make in a pot still. Glasgow and Edinburgh, as well as London and Liverpool, embraced the new technology.

The Irish, meanwhile, were distracted by a tragedy that would haunt the country for years and have a curious knock-on effect on the fortunes of Irish whiskey. In 1845 blight ravaged the potato crop, and the native Irish population, which depended on it for survival, was decimated. A million died and the country started to haemorrhage people.

The prime minister, Robert Peel, fought stiff opposition to repeal the protectionist Corn Laws. Eventually he succeeded, and American maize began steaming its way across the Atlantic and into starving Ireland. Soon this cheap grain was being put to other uses. The canny Scots fed it to their hungry Coffey stills, which until now had lived on a diet of expensive malted barley. The price of grain spirit was now in free fall.

Up until the middle of the nineteenth century, the Scottish industry consisted of nearly 200 small pot still distilleries, producing highly individual, highly flavoured malt whisky. Outside Scotland, this 'highland malt' was almost unheard of – French brandy and Irish whiskey, particularly the Dublin variety, were the drinks of polite society.

Below: In 1849, as Queen Elizabeth visited Belfast, Dublin and Cork, *Punch* published the cartoon 'The New Irish Still', which illustrated the common British delusion that only exertion and the avoidance of whiskey were needed to lift Ireland out of famine.

THE NEW IRISH STILL.

SHOWING HOW ALL SORTS OF GOOD THINGS MAY BE OBTAINED (BY INDUSTRY) OUT OF PEAT.

It is therefore safe to assume that the Irish weren't worried when a change in the law allowed, for the first time, whiskey to be stored in a bonded warehouse, with the tax payable on shipment. Even with the benefit of hindsight, it is hard to see the seeds of the destruction of the Irish industry in that sentence. But it changed everything.

Merchants were now free to buy, blend and bottle their own whiskeys without facing the front-end cost of taxation. The famous Scottish names of Andrew Bell, Alexander Walker and William Teacher are still with us, but they were not distillers – they were local grocers, who combined the Protestant work ethic with Victorian flair and became 'whisky barons'. Using the principles learned from blending tea, these merchants diluted pungent highland malt with spirit from column stills. In this way they could consistently produce a light end product, relatively cheaply and in large quantities.

If the ripples of what was happening in Scotland reached the Dublin whiskey families, it didn't change their way of thinking. It is clear from a book entitled *Truths about Whisky*, published by the Dublin dynasties in 1878, that they were not Luddites – they simply did not believe that 'silent spirit' was, or could ever be, whiskey: 'Good, bad, or indifferent; but it cannot be Whisky, and it ought not to be sold under that name.'

Above: One of the many brands of blended Scotch whisky that flourished during the whisky boom.
Below: A bonded warehouse in Glasgow, which gives some idea of the scale of the Scotch whisky boom.

The Patent Still

In the race for the holy grail of continuous distillation, there were many also-rans, with inventions by Saint Marc, Stein, Cellier-Blumenthal, Perrier and Wright among many variations on the theme. These stills all produced a highly alcoholic spirit by a continuous process, as opposed to the traditional batch method used with copper pot stills.

The term 'patent still' comes from the fact that these designs were protected by patents. Early patent stills were made of a bizarre combination of materials, from iron to wood to stone. However, they soon included copper in their make up, as Barnard noted in his visit to Yoker Distillery, near Glasgow: 'The analyser of the No 2 Coffey's Patent Still is made of copper, and not of wood as is generally the case.'

Over time, Coffey's more efficient model became the standard continuous, patent or column still – nowadays the terms are interchangeable.

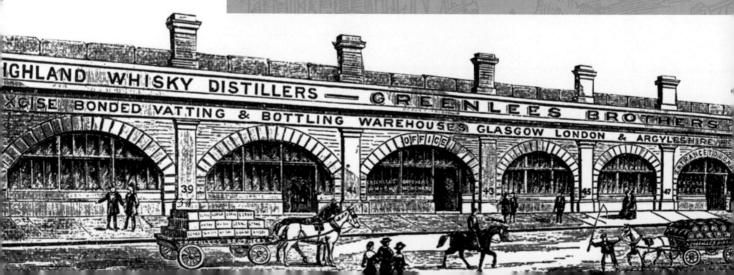

5 . THE GOLDEN YEARS

'The conduct of the Government in allowing an inferior Scotch spirit to be sold as genuine Irish whisky was as bad as that of the people who painted sparrows and then sold them as canaries.'

Mr O'Sullivan MP, in the House of Commons, London, 26 June 1874

The Dublin whiskey families had become victims of their own success. This was an age of almost unfettered free enterprise, and there was no Trade Descriptions Act. Fraud and counterfeit were rife. Irish, and particularly Dublin, whiskey was the Rolex of the late nineteenth century – if you were going to counterfeit something, you might as well go for the big brands, like John Jameson & Son. 'JJ&S' stamped on a barrel, or a Dublin export permit, was as good as money in the bank, regardless of the whiskey's origin. In this laissez-faire market, whiskey distilled in Scottish pot stills, or silent spirit from Liverpool, could and did sell as 'premium Irish whiskey'.

Above: The 'JJ&S' logo stamped on screw caps, in the North Mall bottling plant, Cork.

While their good names were being tarnished by counterfeit whiskey and their markets were being flooded with cheap blends, the big four Dublin distillers sat immobile, convinced that the patent still fad would pass. However, larger forces were at work. Between 1840 and 1860 the number of distilleries in Ireland had halved, although, thanks largely to the Coffey still, output remained stable at around 7,000,000 gallons.

As the smaller regional distilleries closed, others expanded to fill the gap, becoming some of the biggest in the kingdom. At their peak in the late Victorian era, Andrew Watt of Derry and George Roe of Dublin between them produced more whiskey than all of the rural distilleries put together. In Bandon, County Cork, Allman's Distillery boasted six-storey warehouses and its own railway line.

Ireland's railway network was a major factor in these changes to the whiskey industry. By the middle of the century, the train network connected distilleries as far-flung as Midleton in the south, Galway in the west and Bushmills in the north. Whiskey, once sold only locally, could now reach the four corners of the empire.

Those companies that survived the dual onslaught of temperance and famine staged a heroic comeback towards the end of the nineteenth century, and basked in the warm glow of a whiskey boom. If the years

RETURNED EMPTY.
CARRIAGE PAID.
For **JOHN LOCKE & CO.,** Ltd.,
BRUSNA DISTILLERY,
KILBEGGAN.
Via Dublin & Grand Canal.

From

Above: The carpenters' shop
in Power's John's Lane
Distillery, Dublin, c.1920.

between 1779 and 1823 were the glory days for illegal *poitín*, then, despite the Coffey still, fraud and counterfeit, these last few decades of the nineteenth century were the golden years for Irish whiskey.

Just as the blenders were learning their trade, the Irish whiskey industry got a huge boost from, of all people, Mother Nature. A tiny insect, *Phylloxera vastatrix*, or the American grape louse, crossed the Atlantic and proceeded to wipe out the vineyards of the Cognac region. By the 1880s, French brandy was almost impossible to find, and Irish whiskey capitalised on the disaster.

Between 1823 and 1900, the amount of whiskey distilled in Ireland quadrupled, and it was the towns with access to the sea that really felt the boom. Belfast, Cork and Derry became major centres of production and export, but Dublin eclipsed them all, not only for the scale of its distilleries, but for their reputation.

Dublin, with its six distilleries, dominated not only the Irish but the world stage. Of the big four, George Roe and Son of Thomas Street was the largest in the country, covering a massive seventeen acres and with an annual output of 2,000,000 gallons.

John Jameson of Smithfield was also a massive operation, employing 300 men; Sir John Power's distillery had five massive engine rooms; the William

Jameson plant had a cooperage that extended over an acre, and employed thirty men. Jones Road, the smallest of the city-centre operations, not only had its own cooperage, but also stables, blacksmiths' and carpenters' shops, a printing plant, a malt house and duty-free warehouses. It produced 560,000 gallons of whiskey a year and was entirely powered by water.

Tellingly, the sixth and final Dublin distillery, the new state-of-the-art Phoenix Park Distillery in Chapelizod, was owned and operated by the Scottish Distillers Company Limited.

Distillers Company Limited

In 1877 competition in the Scottish grain whisky market gave way to cartel. Six of the largest grain distilleries, between them controlling over seventy-five percent of Britain's grain whisky industry, amalgamated to form the Distillers Company Limited (DCL).

Despite all of the efforts and technological advances of Scottish distilleries, the Irish still dominated the industry – so much so that some Scottish distillers resorted to adding unmalted barley to their mash bill to

Below: DCL's Phoenix Park Distillery, Chapelizod, Dublin.

make 'Irish-style whiskey of the Dublin variety'. DCL were large enough to go one better, and within a year of formation, they were buying into Ireland. 'There is no Patent Still on the Premises,' boasted a DCL trade circular of their new plant at Phoenix Park. 'It is the determination of this company to make the finest Dublin whisky.'

However, DCL had bought into Irish whiskey as the industry was reaching its zenith, and blended Scotch was getting set to conquer the world. The Phoenix Park distillery proved to be a poor investment for DCL, as the days of Ireland's domination of the whiskey world were numbered.

Low tide at Sandymount Strand, Dublin Bay.

Alfred Barnard

Most of what we know about the industry of this period is due to the efforts of one man – Alfred Barnard, who, in 1887, published an account of his visits to each of the 161 whiskey distilleries in the United Kingdom of Great Britain and Ireland.

Barnard visited twenty-eight distilleries in Ireland at a time when two out of every three bottles of whiskey sold by London whiskey merchants Gilbey's was Irish. The British Empire was booming, the drink of choice was Irish, and Dublin whiskey (they had taken to spelling it with an 'e' to help distinguish their product from rural competitors) was the premium brand. Barnard was capturing an industry at its prime; it seemed as if there was no end to the demand for quality Irish.

We don't know how long it took Alfred Barnard to visit and chronicle the 129 Scottish, twenty-eight Irish and four English whiskey distilleries, nor do we know who his travelling companions were. But Barnard evidently enjoyed himself, as a couple of years later he took it upon himself to compile *The Noted Breweries of Great Britain and Ireland*, which runs to four volumes. A tough job I guess, but someone had to do it.

Barnard's verbose style is typical of the Victorian era. Here he describes his arrival in Dublin:

'Soon after passing the Hill of Howth, on which there is a splendid lighthouse, we entered the River Liffey, and found ourselves rapidly approaching the Irish Capital. On arrival at the North Wall we disembarked, when we beheld a sight which caused us much merriment. Jaunting cars rattled up to the wharf one after the other, their drivers arrayed in an assortment of garments from every old clothes shop in the kingdom. Corpulent men with garments so small that no efforts could bring together, and thin men with attire so large, that two or three could be embraced in their covering. 'These "jehus" are as sharp as needles; we were amused to see their quickness in singling out new comers with soft hearts, offering to drive them to all sorts of distant places for the smallest of fares. We secured one of the best of the shabby looking cars, and although the horse was somewhat gone in the legs, he rattled us along so fast that some of us had to hold on to the straps, to prevent being pitched into the dusty street, and we were quite thankful to reach the Gresham Hotel and dismiss our vehicle.'

THE F

ALL AND RISE

TRIALS, TRIBULATIONS AND REBIRTH

1. 'WHAT IS WHISKEY?'

'The patent still is a box of tricks.'
James Power, Dublin distiller, 1908

The latter decades of the nineteenth century had seen an unprecedented and unchecked explosion in the whiskey trade. Thanks to the Coffey still, Scotland was drowning in a 'whisky loch', and lurking in its dark waters was the monster of overproduction. Irish column stills in Limerick and Dundalk were aggravating the problem by dumping grain whiskey on the open market, undercutting DCL and destroying whatever chance the Scottish giant had of controlling supply.

Competition, the lifeblood of Victorian society, had now become, in the words of an internal DCL document, 'destabilising and destructive'. In an attempt to stifle it and fix prices, DCL formed the short-lived United Kingdom Distillers Association (UKDA), commonly known as 'The Whisky Parliament'. All of Ireland's patent whiskey distilleries joined: Murphy of Midleton, Watt of Derry, Brown of Dundalk and Walker of Limerick. They

Pages 42–43: James Cassidy's Distillery at Monasterevin, County Kildare, is still remarkably intact, despite the best part of a century's neglect.
These pages: Barrels at the Jameson Bow Street Distillery, Dublin, *c.*1920.

had little choice – the gun to their heads was DCL's Phoenix Park plant, which, although a pot still distillery, could easily be converted to produce grain spirit, thus flooding the Irish market.

But the Irish were never ones for playing by the rules. The establishment of two maverick grain plants at Avoniel and Connswater in Belfast, both operating outside the whisky parliament, meant that the days of the cartel were numbered. In 1888 the Cork Distilleries Company withdrew from the UKDA and the association collapsed.

The Bubble Bursts

The whiskey bubble finally burst in 1898, eleven years after Barnard's pilgrimage around the United Kingdom, when the Scottish blending firm of Pattison's went spectacularly bust. The brothers Robert and Walter Pattison had a stable of three main whiskeys, two brands of Scotch and an Irish blend, the 'Dew of Slievemore'. But they had been trading fraudulently, buying their own stock to inflate its value and funding the whole venture on credit. When the brothers' business eventually collapsed, they owed £500,000 – an enormous sum at the time. The Pattison bankruptcy sent shock waves through the industry, and the price of whiskey crashed.

The twentieth century dawned and brought with it recession. The ending of the Boer War in South Africa saw the Victorian boom turn into an Edwardian slump. Irish and Scottish warehouses were awash with whiskey, most of it column-still grain, now worth a fraction of its value of a year earlier. As banks called in loans, blenders and distillers went to the wall.

DCL boss William Ross had learned his lesson: there was no future in loose trade associations. The only way to control the market was to exert some muscle. In 1902 the company began to pursue a new policy of slash and burn. DCL went on a buying spree, offering shelter both to large grain distilleries and small pot-still operations. But no sooner was the ink on the contracts dry, than Ross set about winding the distilleries down. In 1900 there were fifteen patent-still distilleries in Scotland; by 1922 DCL had bought all except one.

Ireland too was targeted, and in 1902 Archibald Walker was the first to jump ship and grab the Ross life preserver. Walker, the only man ever to own distilleries in England, Scotland and Ireland, sold out early and joined the board of DCL. His Thomond Gate Distillery in Limerick closed soon afterwards.

Above: John Jameson, the founder of the Jameson Whiskey dynasty. Below: A photograph of Dundalk Distillery dating from the late nineteenth century.

More than anything else, the fortunes of the Phoenix Park Distillery illustrate Irish whiskey's spectacular fall from grace. Just twenty-one years after opening, DCL's Dublin plant went from making Dublin whiskey to producing industrial alcohol, as the pot stills were scrapped and column stills installed. But even this measure wasn't enough to save DCL's Irish operation, and in 1921 it closed forever.

Legislation

In less than a generation, the Coffey still had completely changed the face of the whiskey industry. Technology had sped ahead of legislation and, after the collapse of the Pattison empire, the pointed debate as to exactly what constituted whiskey was back on the agenda.

'Many hold that the pot still product matured and ripened by age is the only spirit that should be designated "whiskey",' wrote William P Coyne in the official handbook for the Irish Pavilion at the Glasgow International Exhibition of 1901. It was all just a matter of opinion, and there were many differing opinions.

In 1890 a legal definition of what constituted 'whiskey' couldn't be agreed upon. The best the Select Committee on British and Foreign Spirits could come up with was: 'Whiskey is certainly a spirit consisting of alcohol and water.' This gave the patent still operators a licence to sell whatever they wanted, as long as their spirits met the additional test that they be 'pure and contain no noxious ingredients'.

So when, in 1905, the London Borough of Islington won a court case by proving that two publicans had acted fraudulently in selling a bottle containing ninety percent one-year-old silent spirit as whiskey, the industry was rocked.

'I must hold,' went the magistrate's judgement, 'that by Irish or Scotch whisky is now meant a spirit obtained in the same methods by the aid of the form of still known as the pot still.' In other words, patent-still spirit was not whiskey. A legal precedent had been set, and the Dublin distillers breathed a sigh of relief, while panic gripped the blending firms in Belfast and Glasgow.

For DCL the ruling was a disaster. Overnight, the whole future of the industry had been thrown into doubt. William Ross argued that the subject was far too important to be decided by the courts and pressed for a royal commission of inquiry to decide, once and for all, exactly 'what is whiskey?'

Above: James Power, founder of John Power & Son Distillery. Opposite: Sunset on the River Liffey near Chapelizod, Dublin.

'The Liffey at Chapel-izod is a beautiful clear stream, and quite unlike the Liffey at Dublin City. Its banks are finely diversified and display sylvan scenes of great beauty.'

Alfred Barnard, 1887

In February 1908, as the royal commission on 'Whiskey and other Potable Spirits' sat for the first time, Ross took his argument to the public. A full-page advertisement in the *Daily Mail* advertised Cambus pure grain whisky. 'Not a Headache in a Gallon,' ran the rather dubious tag line, but the public responded favourably. Irish author and excise man Maurice Walsh, who went on to pen *The Quiet Man*, was impressed with what he tasted. 'Cambus on the Forth,' he wrote, 'was held to be the best of the patent distilleries, its only rival being Chapelizod on the Liffey.' Both were DCL plants.

For seventeen long months the arguments raged in the royal commission. Should there be a minimum period of maturation? What constituted Irish whiskey? Could grain whiskey even be called 'whiskey'? In the end, the commission was 'unable to recommend that the use of the word whiskey should be restricted to spirit manufactured by the pot still process.' In other words, the patent distillers had won the day. Whiskey was whiskey whether it came from a pot or a Coffey still. For the Irish purists this was the worst of all possible outcomes – DCL were now free to blend whatever they wanted, in whatever quantities they required. There was worse to come.

In 1909 David Lloyd George, the Welsh teetotaller and chancellor of the exchequer, increased the tax on whiskey by thirty-three percent, while beer and wine were left untouched. Sales collapsed as the cold wind of recession blew through these islands.

As the world tumbled towards the Great War, Wexford, Limavady, Lower Comber and Galway distilleries shut for the last time. These four minnows had floundered under the combined weight of taxation, recession and competition, as the big boys in Dublin and Belfast worked harder to stay afloat.

Christmas 1914 came and went and, contrary to popular expectation, the war in Europe didn't end. In fact it got worse, as both sides dug themselves in. 'Drink,' declared Lloyd George, 'is doing more damage in the war than all the German submarines put together.' He proposed nothing short of total prohibition, something that the Irish Nationalists, who held the balance of power in parliament, would not hear of. The distilling industry was just too important to the Irish economy.

In 1916 a compromise was reached that, to this day, still shapes the way we consume whiskey. Now whiskey could no longer be sold straight from the still – it had to be matured for at least three years, and it had to be sold at a minimum alcoholic strength. Pub opening hours were also to be

Below: An advertisement for Cambus, the world's first bottling of a single grain whiskey.

Above: Delivery vans outside the Kilbeggan Distillery in the 1940s.

controlled. For once, things were working out for the pot still whiskey companies – they already matured their whiskey, while the patent still operators did not.

Next, to conserve grain for food, distilling was banned for the year 1917–18. Not surprisingly, the price of Irish whiskey rose. The market was now so buoyant that John Jameson and Son were only able to send their London agent Gilbey's half of their order. When distilling was allowed to restart in 1919, the confident distillers laid down huge stocks of spirit to mature.

But it was a false confidence and a terrible error of judgement. By the mid-1920s, when this whiskey was ready to sell, the market and the country had changed beyond recognition.

Labels of the Period

Dublin whiskey, particularly that of John Jameson & Son, was always considered to be the premium brand. In 1904, 18/– would buy a gallon of 'Old Irish Whiskey' from Mitchell's of Dublin, with no mention of any particular distillery. For an extra shilling you could get a gallon of ten-year-old DWD whiskey. However, a gallon of 'JJ&S, guaranteed pure and of the age stated,' of the same vintage would set you back a stiff 24/–. It is therefore not surprising that some merchants resorted to using labels, like the one on the right, second from the top, which bore more than a passing resemblance to the real thing.

In an attempt to discourage imitators and counterfeiters, John Jameson & Son took to numbering and watermarking their labels and adopted the term 'Dublin whiskey'. John Power & Son went a step further and, instead of following the customary practice of selling all of their produce to merchants, started limited distillery bottling in 1886. They issued white labels to merchants and adopted a gold label, similar to the familiar modern one shown on the right, for their own distillery bottlings.

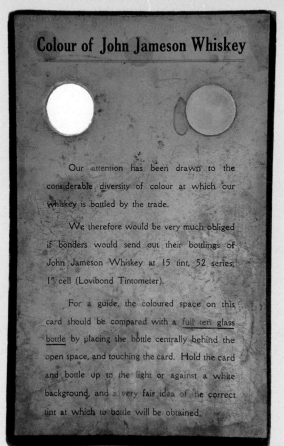

Colour of John Jameson Whiskey

Our attention has been drawn to the considerable diversity of colour at which our whiskey is bottled by the trade.

We therefore would be very much obliged if bonders would send out their bottlings of John Jameson Whiskey at 15 tint, 52 series, 1" cell (Lovibond Tintometer).

For a guide, the coloured space on this card should be compared with a full ten glass bottle by placing the bottle centrally behind the open space, and touching the card. Hold the card and bottle up to the light or against a white background, and a very fair idea of the correct tint at which to bottle will be obtained.

Above: In an attempt to standardise the colour of Jameson whiskey bottled by the bonded trade, Jameson issued this colour correction chart. By holding a sample behind the hole on the left, bonders could then check the colour of their whiskey against the standard colour disc on the right. Lighter whiskey could then be darkened with caramel.

This radical departure was meant to ensure that the public got what they paid for, as some unscrupulous landlords were not averse to topping up their Powers with cheaper provincial whiskey.

The modern bottle of Irish whiskey is therefore a pretty recent innovation. Glass bottles were expensive to produce and bottling was very labour-intensive. Distillers preferred to pass this expense on to middlemen – the whiskey bonders – leaving them free to focus not on selling, but on distilling. This policy of selling through middlemen, who in turn sold the whiskey direct from the cask, proved a real problem to the Irish as branding became more and more important.

In the early part of the twentieth century, with distilleries bottling mostly for export, Irish whiskey bonders started bottling whiskey for the domestic market. In order to enhance their own reputation, they would put their name on the label, often not mentioning the distillery, or giving it just a passing reference.

It was whiskey merchants like Mitchell's of Belfast who first adopted the now universal practice of branding. Whiskeys like 'Cruiskeen Lawn' gave no indication of what was in the bottle or where it came from. This was unimportant – Mitchell's were selling a brand, and doing so with a lot more panache than other smaller merchants like Corry's of Kilrush.

Redbreast, Green Spot and Crock of Gold were other big brands owned not by distilleries, but by bonders. This further reduced the power of the Irish producers, already struggling to keep up with advancing sales of Scotch on international markets.

2 . DECIMATION

'Ireland sober, Ireland free.'

Nationalist battle-cry

In the middle of the First World War (1914–18), rebellion once again gripped Ireland, in the form of the 1916 Easter Rising. This was followed by the War of Independence (1919–21), which in turn was followed by the bloody Civil War (1922–23). Ireland went into the twentieth century with a booming economy, an almost seamless part of the Great British Empire. In a little over twenty years the whole thing had unravelled, as the agricultural boom collapsed, prices slumped and the country was partitioned. In the south the Irish Free State was founded, while six of Ireland's Ulster counties remained part of the United Kingdom.

Above: An IRA flying column in Connemara during the War of Independence in 1921.

55

By 1911, Dundalk Distillery was struggling for survival, dumping its whiskey on the London market. Smelling blood, William Ross started to circle, and within a year DCL had bought out the company. It was the shape of things to come.

In 1920, while the Irish were busy fighting each other, the Scottish Johnnie Walker, Dewar's and Buchanan's Black & White were already established global brands, being sold in over 120 countries. In 1925 Distillers Company Limited acquired all three, further strengthening its hold on the international market. Aggressive selling of a lighter whisky had paid off for the Scots, who recognised the value of a strong brand identity. No Irish distillery could approach their level of marketing sophistication.

Meanwhile domestic demand, on which the Irish industry depended for survival, had collapsed. In the brave new world of the Irish Free State, the Irish distillers found themselves out in the cold. They were, according to Minister for Finance Ernest Blythe, 'the dregs of landlordism'. This was a cheap shot aimed at Andrew Jameson, the fifth-generation Jameson now running the distillery. He was also a senator, heavily involved in the Irish Pot Still Distillers Association and a staunch Unionist to boot. For a time he also had the dubious honour of being number one on the Republican hit list of senators to be shot on sight. Whatever about Andrew Jameson's politics, the fact is that every distillery in the Free State was operated by an Irish family: in Dublin there were the Jamesons and Powers; in the midlands the Lockes and the Williams; and in Cork the Murphys. But there was no political will to help the industry. The State and the distillers were deadlocked, with the government seeing the industry as 'a source of very substantial revenue,' and nothing more.

Right: The staff of Power's John's Lane Distillery, 1924. In the centre, wearing the top hat, is Sir Thomas Talbot Power, Proprietor.

In the brave new world of the Irish Free State,
the Irish distillers found themselves out in the cold.

Lips that touch Whiskey

are lips that will Never touch Mine

WOMEN'S CHRISTIAN TEMPERANCE UNION

Even the Dublin giants were not immune to the policies of a government who saw whiskey as a 'Unionist industry'. The recession was now biting hard, with distillers selling fifteen-year-old whiskey at seven-year-old prices to a shrinking domestic market. With the introduction of Prohibition in 1919, the growing American market evaporated overnight, while after partition in 1921, trade with Britain and her colonies became increasingly difficult.

'Yet another nail is being driven into the coffin of the long-abused Union,' commented the in-house *DCL Gazette*, as the Free State erected trade barriers designed to raise revenue and help native industry. The Edinburgh-based company was finding it harder and harder to operate in what was now a foreign country. In 1923, three years after the closure of its Phoenix Park operation, DCL's strike-ridden Dundalk Distillery, which had been bought in 1912, also fell silent.

The mighty Ulster distilleries of Waterside and Abbey Street in Derry, and Connswater and Avoniel in Belfast, had amalgamated in 1902, to form United Distilleries Limited. They believed there was strength in unity, and hoped to take on William Ross. But it wasn't to be. By 1922 the strategy had flopped, and they too were taken over by DCL, which welcomed them to a 'large and united family, with but one object, the real good of that family itself'.

The two Derry firms were closed in 1925. A year later, fire gutted Connswater and it never reopened. Its patent still was moved across the water to DCL's Hammersmith plant, where it ended its days making gin. Reduced to manufacturing yeast, Avoniel Distillery hung on the longest, but in the end, according to a DCL document, 'transport costs to the highly competitive yeast market in Great Britain told against Avoniel.' In May 1929, DCL shut the plant down. Ross had finally locked the door and thrown away the key on distilling on the island of Ireland. The Scottish industry had fallen on hard times and the 'good of that family' required that any surplus capacity be ruthlessly cut. In a couple of decades, DCL had managed to close seven Irish distilleries, including all but one of the island's grain stills.

Dublin distillers also sought strength in numbers. In 1891 William Jameson and George Roe joined forces with Jones Road, forming Dublin Whiskey Distillers (DWD). Jameson and Roe were two of the big four Dublin distilleries (the other two, John Jameson and John Power, as we shall see, were also far from the peak of fiscal health). In theory DWD could not fail, but this is exactly what happened; the first two firms closed in 1923, with Jones Road closing three years later, though some distilling did continue at the plant until 1942.

Below: An advertisement for Tullamore Dew which still graces the town.

Give every man his Dew

The Brewery Tap

The decimation continued in Cork. Of the five companies that had amalgamated to form the Cork Distilleries Company (CDC) in 1867, the Green and Daly's of John Street were the first two to close, within years of forming CDC. A fire at the North Mall plant in 1920 saw it close too, though the buildings are still used today by the Irish Distillers Group as a bottling plant. The Watercourse closed in the 1910s, leaving only Midleton.

The two Cork companies that remained outside CDC fared little better. Allman's sold their Bandon distillery to the brewers Beamish in 1913. It ceased production in 1925, as did the city's other independent firm, the Glen Distillery at Kilnap.

In the midlands, the smaller family firms were also disappearing. Birr Distillery in County Offaly burned to the ground in 1889, and there would be no phoenix from the ashes. This was the first of the places visited by Barnard to close. In 1898 the even more obscure Banagher Distillery shut down. It had been mothballed when Barnard toured Ireland, and so little is known about it. Cassidy's of Monasterevin survived into the twentieth century, but went into voluntary liquidation in 1921. It would never reopen.

With Ireland's only native industry in ruins, all taoiseach William Cosgrave could muster was: 'It would be a pity if the pot still business went out of existence,' but neither he nor his government did anything to save it. By the time he left power in 1932, the Free State's five remaining distilleries were all in tatters.

The two small midlands firms of Locke's in Kilbeggan and Williams's in Tullamore had managed to hang on, but only by mothballing their entire operation for long periods of time. Between 1924 and 1931 Kilbeggan was closed, while Tullamore was shut for thirteen long years, from 1925 to 1937. It is a minor miracle that they ever reopened.

By the 1930s, Midleton was distilling for only two brief weeks in a year.

In the north, after DCL had closed down all the opposition, there were just three small pot still companies left, which posed no threat to anybody – Bushmills, Upper Comber and Coleraine.

This left Dunville's Royal Irish Distillery in Belfast as the only substantial distillery in Ulster. During the 1920s, Dunville's had expanded into the gaps left by the closure of the other Ulster plants, and ended the decade in profit. However, in a bizarre twist, the company approached DCL in the mid-1930s, asking to be taken over as a going concern. William Ross was not interested, and the board of the Royal Irish Distillery voted themselves out of existence, evidently convinced that there was no future in Irish whiskey. It is hard to believe that while still making a profit, Dunville's pulled down the shutters and simply gave up. This sums up the despair running through what, thirty years earlier, had been the greatest distilling industry in the world.

As the 1930s drew to a close and the world was once more consumed by war, DCL announced that 'Ireland had become an irrelevance', and disposed of all of their remaining Irish whiskey by redistilling it for industrial use.

Below: Warehouses at the Tullamore Distillery, County Offaly, in the early 1950s.

One of Many – Allman's of Bandon

The list of Irish distilleries that closed in the early years of the twentieth century is long and distinguished. Time has moved on, and most of these once household names are now long forgotten. Yet each of these plants employed hundreds of people, often in areas with little or no other industry, and each of those people had a story.

If you follow in Barnard's footsteps and use your imagination, it is possible to get an idea of the scale of the industry in its Victorian prime. Sometimes, as in the case of Kilbeggan, it is as if time has stood still, but more often than not all you will see are crumbling warehouses and new housing estates. My heart cannot help but sink every time I pass through Bandon, for although the Allman family house still stands high on a hill overlooking the town, their distillery has literally vanished.

Today the town of Bandon lies an easy half-hour drive southwest of Cork city. In Barnard's day, travel to 'this fine distillery' was by steam train, and the distillery had its own siding. Two hundred men worked at Allman's. The malthouse was second in size only to that of Guinness's in Dublin, and in the newest of the sites' fifteen warehouses, each of the three floors measured a quarter of an acre.

In a way, the story of this distillery is representative of the entire struggle of the Irish industry. The company was a good employer, it produced well-respected whiskeys and it resisted change. In 1904, at the age of eighty-two, James C Allman became the company's senior manager. James C, like most of his contemporaries, didn't believe that the Coffey still had a future, and banned its introduction into Bandon. This brought him into direct conflict with company director JJ McDaniel, who was also his nephew.

In 1910 James C went to the High Court to have the partnership dissolved. The court ordered that the company be wound up, the proceeds to be divided equally among the shareholders. However, James C died in December of that year, before the company could be closed down. As all his shares passed to his three nephews, JJ now found himself to be the majority shareholder. He had no intention of closing down the distillery.

A slowdown in sales, combined with huge court costs, crippled JJ, and his plans to introduce a Coffey still never materialised. In 1915 he lost control of the company to Cork brewers Beamish. A decade later distilling ceased, with 500,000 gallons of whiskey left maturing in the Allman warehouses.

It is hard to believe, but it took over a decade to dispose of the whiskey.

The site was sold in 1939 to a firm of Cork builders. The magnificent buildings were levelled, a cattle mart being built on the site. Today only two bottles of Allman's whiskey are known to exist, housed in the local museum along with a selection of tools and pottery crocks from the distillery.

The loss of Allman's crippled the west Cork town, just as the loss of the Wexford, Galway, Birr, Monasterevin, Limerick, Dundalk and Limavady distilleries sent tremors through local communities the length and breadth of the island. Over the next decades, as blended Scotch swept the world, trades such as coopering and boilermaking would almost entirely disappear. And over the next thirty years, the whole industry would almost follow them into oblivion.

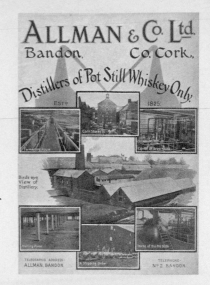

Above: An advertisement from a trade journal published early in the nineteenth century, and reproduced here for the first time. The phone number supplied is 'Bandon 2', Bandon 1 would have been the police station, and it is highly unlikely that Bandon 3 even existed.

Below: One of the few known photographs of Allman's Distillery in Bandon, taken in 1905. It is clear that things hadn't changed much since Barnard's day.

3. FROM BAD TO WORSE

'O long life to the man who invented potheen
Sure the Pope ought to make him a martyr
If myself was this moment Victoria, our Queen,
I'd drink nothing but whiskey and wather.'

Zozimus (1794–1846), 'In Praise of Potheen'

On the American east coast in the early 1900s, Irish whiskey was sold at a premium. However, with the advent of US congressman Andrew J Volstead's 'noble experiment' of Prohibition in 1919, it all but disappeared from the landscape of the Irish-American community. There were still plenty of Irish-Americans, and therefore 'Irish' was a popular drink to bootleg. If you were lucky, the 'Irish' served in a speakeasy teapot wouldn't kill you, but its aroma owed less to the 'auld sod' than it did to tobacco or even boot polish, while the colour didn't come from oak ageing, but from Dr Pepper.

At the height of Prohibition, the city of New York alone had 30,000

An aerial view of Jameson's Bow Street Distillery, c.1920. The famous Jameson chimney to the right now has a viewing platform on top, and is open to the public.

65

speakeasies, all serving 'bathtub gin' or 'whiskey'. Al Capone and other mobsters produced most of their own alcohol, as quickly and as cheaply as possible. Favourite shortcuts included pumping the wash through a car radiator and adding battery acid. Lead absorbed from old radiators could cause paralysis, brain damage or even death.

Needless to say, bootlegging did very little for the reputation of Irish whiskey, but the attitude of the Dublin distillers didn't help. In the 1920s, Joe Kennedy (father of John F Kennedy) approached both Jameson's and Power's with a speculative 'post-Prohibition' order for whiskey. Though both companies could have done with the work, they declined, as accepting the business would be conniving to break the law. Joe Kennedy then approached the Scots, who had no problem filling his order.

Ever the entrepreneurs, the Scottish distillers would never let Prohibition get in the way of good business. Not only did they plan for the abolition of Prohibition, but they ignored it while it was there. The Scots exploited a loophole that allowed heavily peated malts to be imported for 'medicinal' uses; they also designed brands specifically for the Prohibition market.

At the height of the 'dry' season in 1923, whiskey blenders the Rudd brothers created the 'Cutty Sark' blend specifically for the American market. Their new whisky was shipped to the Bahamas, then loaded aboard British-registered vessels, which anchored in international waters off New York in

Below: Part of a consignment of 1,000 cases of Jameson whiskey being loaded onto the freighter *American Merchant* in London, for shipment to America. This was the first shipment of Jameson to America after the repeal of Prohibition.

what became known as 'Rum Row'. Some whisky was smuggled in through Canada, where it also found a welcome market. Within a couple of decades, Cutty Sark was the biggest-selling Scotch in the United States.

The Irish whiskey industry was at its lowest ebb when, in 1932, a new government locked horns with London over land duties. This soon snowballed into what became known as the 'Economic War'. Britain, the destination of ninety percent of Irish exports, was now disappearing behind a wall of escalating duties and levies. With the world already in the grip of the Great Depression, protectionism and self-sufficiency became the buzzwords of the day.

In 1933, when Prohibition came to an ignoble end, the Irish whiskey business was in no shape to cash in. The global brand had arrived, and the Irish had missed the boat. Irish distillers blamed their American agents, who in turn blamed the distilleries. But the simple truth was that for too long the Irish had been too complacent.

De Valera and Churchill

After the First World War, both the Irish and the Scottish worked hard to build their share of the US market. However, the outbreak of the Second World War changed everything.

Above left: Eamon de Valera.
Above right: Winston Churchill.

In the early days of what became known in neutral Ireland as 'the Emergency', Eamon de Valera's government capped whiskey exports, initially by half, and then by half again, 'because of the enormous revenue which is derived from whiskey consumed on the home market'. It was the epitome of short-sighted isolationism.

By contrast, Churchill saw Scotch as a source of hard currency. 'On no account reduce the barley for whisky,' he said. 'This takes years to mature and is an invaluable export and dollar producer.' Foreign sales were encouraged, while home consumption was cut back to a quarter. Anyone who has seen the movie *Whisky Galore* will appreciate the drought that engulfed Britain. Scotch became scarcer and scarcer, unless, that is, you were in America.

By 1945 the race to establish dominance in the international market was over. While the Irish were fighting over the scraps, the Scots had conquered America. Restrictions on the export of Irish whiskey continued until 1953, and by then a whole generation had grown up in America never knowing Irish – to them Scotch was whiskey and whiskey was Scotch. The words were, and still are, interchangeable.

Irish Coffee

Above: The flying boat *Yankee Clipper* at Foynes Harbour on the River Shannon.

From the mid-1930s, the fabulously romantic 'flying boats' refuelled at Foynes on the west coast of Ireland before crossing the Atlantic. In 1942 one of these flights turned back due to bad weather. Tired and cold, the passengers were hurried back into the terminal building, where barman Joe Sheridan had created something special. Coffee, sugar, cream and whiskey combined to produce the now-legendary Irish Coffee. It was an immediate success, and the drink has stood the test of time better than the glamorous flying boats or the airport, which were pensioned off in the mid-1940s.

In the early 1950s, journalist Stan DeLaplane from the *San Francisco Chronicle* stopped off at the world's first duty-free airport, across the estuary from Foynes at Shannon. Stan sampled one (or two) Irish coffees and was

captivated. He took the recipe back home to the Buena Vista Café on Fisherman's Wharf and, before long, more Irish whiskey was being drunk in San Francisco than in Ireland. America had gone Irish coffee mad.

To the beleaguered industry this was a real shot in the arm, with Kilbeggan and Tullamore in particular embracing the extra business. But in 1952, the same year that Joe Sheridan went to work stateside at the Buena Vista, the Irish government drove the final nail into the coffins of the midland distilleries. A huge hike in duty saw domestic sales evaporate and the last remaining stills started to close down.

Distilling ceased in Locke's of Kilbeggan in November 1953. At the time of closing, business was so bad that there was enough unsold whiskey in stock to maintain the current level of sales for a hundred years.

A year later Tullamore was again mothballed.

Above: The Buena Vista Café at Fisherman's Wharf, San Francisco, in 1961. No, they're not drinking pints of Guinness, those are all Irish coffees. The café went through 15,000 bottles of Irish whiskey a year.

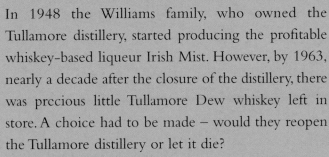

Irish Mist

In 1948 the Williams family, who owned the Tullamore distillery, started producing the profitable whiskey-based liqueur Irish Mist. However, by 1963, nearly a decade after the closure of the distillery, there was precious little Tullamore Dew whiskey left in store. A choice had to be made – would they reopen the Tullamore distillery or let it die?

John Power & Son were approached to see if they would provide the whiskey for Irish Mist. Power's had the whiskey but no international penetration; Tullamore Dew had the latter but not the former. A deal was done, and the fate of the Midland distillery was sealed. In return for the live export brand name 'Tullamore Dew', Power's would provide the whiskey for Irish Mist. The Williams family now had no need to reopen their Tullamore plant and the place was left to rot.

The Republic of Ireland was now down to just three distilleries – John Jameson and John Power in Dublin, and the Cork Distilleries Company plant at Midleton in County Cork.

A hike in UK duty hit the Upper Comber distillery in County Down, which stopped production in 1953, leaving just Bushmills and Coleraine distilleries in Northern Ireland.

The island was now reduced to five distilleries and the Irish coffee boom had proved to be something of a Trojan horse. Scotch was now the sophisticated drink enjoyed by Americans, while Irish was seen as only fit to be drunk on St Patrick's Day, or when smothered in coffee, cream and sugar.

Left: This warehouse on the banks of the Grand Canal in Tullamore now houses the Tullamore Dew Heritage Centre.

4. THE HUGE GAMBLE

'As to the actual process of distilling, we would never depart
from what has been handed down to us.'

Andrew Jameson, in the final report of the Royal Commission on Whiskey, 1909

By the early 1960s, Ireland's remaining distilleries were locked in a battle to the death. The situation was untenable. The Scottish industry was now a global one, while the Irish were fighting it out for a tiny and rapidly shrinking domestic market. Exporting wasn't even an issue: 'If someone wanted whiskey they'd sell it,' remembers John Clement Ryan. 'But the Irish distillers never chased it.'

John Clement Ryan is the last link with Dublin's great distilling dynasties. Prior to his retirement, he was the last member of the Power family to work for Irish Distillers. His father, John Ryan, Managing Director of John Power & Son, first thought the unthinkable sometime in the early 1960s. He saw that a merger of the Republic's three remaining distilleries was the only way the industry could survive. Finally, on 8 March 1966, John Power & Son,

Putting on a united front: Members of the Irish Whiskey and Distillers Association outside Trinity College, Dublin, before their historic sales trip to New York in 1960. Left to Right: Michael O'Reilly (Secretary), Austin Boyd (Bushmills), Major Charles Robinson (Jameson), Ronnie Murphy (CDC), Willam Campbell (Gilbey's), Desmond Williams (Tullamore), John Ryan (Power's).

73

Above: A Powers window
in the Irish Whiskey Corner
in Bow Street, Dublin.

John Jameson & Son and the Cork Distilleries Company put centuries of rivalry behind them and amalgamated. The United Distillers of Ireland (UDI) was born. Shortly afterwards, Rhodesia's Ian Smith announced his country's own UDI (Unilateral Declaration of Independence). Lest there be any confusion between African politics and Irish whiskey, the Irish UDI quickly changed its name to Irish Distillers Limited (IDL).

For two years, for fear of offending any of the founding families, Irish Distillers survived without a managing director. Then in 1968, in a break with a several-hundred-year tradition, a non-family member was appointed to run an Irish distillery. Kevin McCourt had just finished a five-year contract as director general of the newly launched Irish television service, RTÉ. He had clearly learnt from the mistakes of the Dublin Whiskey Distillers (DWD), which had foundered in the early decades of the century. To survive, Irish Distillers could not operate as an alliance of three separate companies. They would have to totally reinvent themselves.

'It was tragic but inescapable,' remembers John Clement Ryan. 'Kevin had to persuade the board to close all the existing distilleries and replace them with one modern one. It was a huge gamble, but it had to be done.'

The changes proposed by McCourt were as radical as they were necessary. Not only was the shape of the industry to change; so too were the whiskeys themselves. After a century of denial, the Irish were to embrace the blend in a big way. By 1975 all production would be relocated to a brand new distillery, costing £9,000,000, to be built behind the old one at Midleton, County Cork. Irish Distillers also stopped the centuries-old practice of selling their whiskey to merchants, and started selling direct to the public.

'When the letter arrived saying they were cutting all links with the bonded whiskey trade, we wanted Kevin McCourt hung, drawn and quartered.' Jonathan Mitchell's family had been whiskey bonders since 1886, and he remembers the passion and anger felt by all in the trade. 'Irish Distillers had recently started bottling Crested Ten, we knew they wanted all the bonder brands dead and that's more or less what happened.'

The horse to which the wagon would be hitched was the new distillery-bottled John Jameson brand. This was signalled as early as 1970. In that year Patrick Campbell, a journalist famous for his stammer as well as for his wit, visited the new bottling plant in Dublin. 'Many of the bottles have a beautifully tapered shape,' he wrote. 'They will contain the new-type Jameson.'

The days of heavy pot still whiskey were numbered, and old brands of Irish were to be reinvented. 'In the tasting room I get the chance to try out the new Jameson,' wrote Campbell. And his verdict? 'Exquisite! Light and airy, fragrant and glowing – like nothing I have ever drunk before. It isn't just a beautiful Irish. It's like a completely new drink that should have a completely new name.' The following year, distilling ceased at the distillery in Bow Street. But the world's love affair with 'Jemie' had begun.

The march into the future was now unstoppable. The brand new distillery was built in the shadow of the old; one Friday night in September 1975, the workers at the Old Midleton plant left the nineteenth century and on Monday morning started work in the twentieth. A year after opening, all links with the past were severed when the Watercourse Distillery in Cork and John's Lane in Dublin, home of John Power and Son since 1791, were closed.

Above: Taken in the early 1960s, this photograph shows the CDC Distillery at Midleton, County Cork, with the Dungourney River in the foreground.

And Then there was One ...

The contraction of the Irish whiskey industry was also felt north of the border. After the closure of Old Comber in the early 1950s, Ulster was left with a mere two distilleries – Coleraine and Bushmills, standing just eight miles apart.

What Coleraine and Bushmills lacked in output, they more than made up for in reputation. The former supplied its famous HC brand to the House of Commons in London and, after 1954, it supplied the grain whiskey for Bushmills blends. In 1947 the distilleries merged and Coleraine's separate identity disappeared.

Bushmills changed hands again in 1964, when Charrington United Breweries of England bought the distillery. This firm of London brewers ran a chain of 5,000 tied pubs. In theory, this should have given Bushmills whiskey enviable access to the British market; however, the practice worked out differently. Distilling was not a core activity of Charrington, and by the early 1970s they were looking to offload the distillery.

'Bushmills was the only distillery in Ireland that was not part of Irish Distillers,' recalls Richard Burrows, former Managing Director of Irish Distillers, who began his career at the Old Bushmills Distillery. 'The logic was that we acquire it. But there was no movement.' Charrington stonewalled the move – Bushmills was for sale, but not to Irish Distillers.

76

The Seagram Vaccination

One morning in 1972, a telephone rang in the Irish Distillers headquarters, beside the old Jameson Distillery in Dublin. On the line was Jack Yogman, President of Seagram, the multinational drinks giant.

The Canadian-based Seagram, at the time worth in excess of $2 billion, was one of the biggest players in the world of whiskey and, as John Clement Ryan puts it, 'They wanted the tiny minnow of Irish Distillers.'

'Seagram wanted to take over Irish Distillers,' confirms Chairman Richard Burrows. 'But we were not for sale.' However, the approach had brought the reality of their situation home to the Irish Distillers board. Irish Distillers was a small company with little or no international presence and, although the Seagram offer had been a friendly one, it was apparent that sooner or later the company would again be targeted. Next time they might not be so lucky.

'The situation was delicate and Kevin McCourt played it beautifully,' says John Clement Ryan. McCourt offered Seagram a chunk of Irish Distillers, and in return he wanted Yogman to deliver the previously unobtainable Old Bushmills Distillery.

Above: John Clement Ryan wouldn't be photographed drinking anything less than Redbreast. 'I have my reputation to think of,' he jokes.

Seagram bought Bushmills from Charrington, and over a four-year period 'exchanged' the distillery for fifteen percent of Irish Distillers. Not only had McCourt secured the County Antrim distillery, but, with the Canadians owning part of Irish Distillers, new markets were now open to Irish whiskey. There was also no way anyone would now try to buy the company. 'It was a vaccination against takeover,' chuckles John Clement Ryan. 'We were a small fish in a big pond. Large fish would sniff us, get a whiff of Seagram and swim a mile.'

With the acquisition of Bushmills, one company now controlled the only three working distilleries on the island – Midleton, Bushmills and Coleraine. Irish Distillers Limited was the Irish whiskey industry.

In 1978 Coleraine's column stills went cold. From then on, Midleton would supply all of the company's grain whiskey needs. There were now just two distilleries on the island, between them producing fifteen whiskeys, four vodkas, two gins and one rum. Over fifty percent of Irish Distillers' sales

White Spirits

Cork Distilleries Company pioneered the move into white spirits in 1941, when it launched Cork Dry Gin, still the largest-selling brand of gin in Ireland. Nordoff vodka followed in 1960.

In 1958 John Power & Son launched their own brand of gin, and in 1960 the wonderfully mock-Russian Sarotov vodka.

Below: The Giant's Causeway, County Antrim.

were in the Republic of Ireland, but on the global market Irish accounted for a mere one percent of whiskey sales.

Even with Seagram on board, Irish Distillers was still no match for DCL. The company simply didn't have the financial muscle to play with the big boys on the international stage. Not one of its products featured in the top 100 global brands. When in 1986, Guinness, a still larger fish, ate DCL, and a year later Seagram decided it wanted to sell its share in Irish Distillers, it was clear that it wouldn't be long before the sharks started circling.

5. MODERN TIMES

The French Connection

By the late 1980s, Seagram's relationship with Irish Distillers hadn't borne fruit. The new markets that Burrows had hoped to tap into remained as elusive as ever, while the Canadians weren't getting much of a return on their investment. Seagram slowly began to offload its shares, and the subsequent struggle for control of Irish Distillers deteriorated into Ireland's biggest and most vicious takeover battle.

On 30 May 1988, soft-drinks company and owners of Irish Mist, Cantrell & Cochrane (owned jointly by Allied-Lyons and Guinness Ireland), and Gilbey's (a subsidiary of Grand Metropolitan and riding high on the success of Bailey's Irish Cream Liqueur) joined forces and bid to take over Irish Distillers. Between them, Allied-Lyons and Grand Metropolitan owned eighteen of the world's top spirit brands. Their ambition was that 'Bushmills and Jameson should join the top 100.'

Above: The old Midleton Distillery, jewel in the crown of Irish Distillers.

The GC&C consortium wanted to break up Irish Distillers and share out the brands, 'thereby ending the monopoly which has existed over the marketing of Irish whiskey since the early 1970s,' as they put it. Gilbey's were to take Jameson, Paddy and Cork Dry Gin, while C&C were to own Tullamore Dew, Bushmills and Powers.

'Apart from anything else, their bid totally undervalued the company,' says Richard Burrows, Managing Director of Irish Distillers at the time. The board, who also didn't want their brands broken up, rejected GC&C's hostile bid of £3.15 a share. Both sides dug in and insults flew around Dublin, C&C managing director Tony O'Brien calling Irish Distillers 'a bloody embarrassment to all of us,' and adding that if Irish Distillers had invented Bailey's, the brand would never have been heard of.

Above: Richard Burrows, joint CEO of Pernod Ricard.

In response, Irish Distillers announced projected record profits, labelled GC&C a cover for an international takeover of Irish whiskey and launched their 'Keep the Spirit Irish' advertising campaign, which in retrospect is ironic, as at the time Burrows was in secret takeover negotiations with the French company Pernod Ricard.

'I'd known Pernod Ricard for years through Austin Nichols, which is part of the group,' says Richard Burrows. Austin Nichols are the makers of Wild Turkey Kentucky whiskey, and at the time handled many Irish Distillers brands in the United States. 'We were finding it difficult to get access to international markets and we were looking for a hook-up. It hadn't worked with Seagram's and, in the face of a hostile bid, Pernod Ricard were making the right noises.'

It was Pernod Ricard who had approached Irish Distillers, not the other way around. Initially the French were only interested in taking a share of the company, but when Thierry Jacquillat of Pernod Ricard flew into Dublin, Burrows floated the idea of the French company taking total control of Irish Distillers.

Around the same time, the GC&C partnership ran into problems when the EC declared that their bid was potentially in breach of European competition law. Grand Metropolitan, under the guise of Gilbey's (who kept the GC&C name), decided to go it alone, and made a 'final offer' of £4 a share. But it was a misjudged move. 'If GC&C had bid around £4.20, moved into the market and bought up all the shares they could get their hands on, it would have been all over. The bidders would have secured Irish

Distillers within a matter of days,' a 'key figure' is quoted as saying at the time.

In hesitating, GC&C 'left the door open', according to this source. Thierry Jacquillat got the approval of the Pernod Ricard board for a friendly takeover, and within a fortnight the French drinks giant had agreed to take over Irish Distillers for £4.50 a share.

The battle for control of Irish Distillers quickly deteriorated into open warfare, fought in the press and in the courts. Eventually the Department of Industry and Commerce gave Pernod Ricard the go-ahead to complete the deal, and the battle was over. Grand Metropolitan sold its 29.9% holding in Irish Distillers to Pernod Ricard, and the five Irish directors resigned.

With a single contract, the French had gained control of almost the entire Irish whiskey industry. Almost, but not quite, for on a peninsula in County Louth, a pair of whiskey stills that had been cold for nearly forty years had spluttered back to life.

The Whiskey Raid of Cooley

'I was on a plane at the time returning from Manila,' says Dr John Teeling. 'I read the place was for sale and I bought it site unseen. It's the only way to do it.' The year was 1987, and the Irish Government were selling the Ceimicí Teoranta (Chemicals Limited) plant on the Cooley peninsula, County Louth.

In the isolationist 1930s, five industrial alcohol factories were set up by the State. The Ceimicí Teoranta plants were scattered across the country in areas of high unemployment. The idea was to turn diseased potatoes into a product with the wonderful moniker Power Methylated Spirits (PMS). By law, petrol companies operating in Ireland had to mix PMS with their motor fuel.

By the early 1980s, PMS was a thing of the past. The Cooley plant had diversified into making potable spirits, which found their way into brands like Smirnoff vodka and Bailey's Irish Cream liqueur. But state involvement in commercial enterprises was now very much out of vogue and the government had no option but to sell off the Cooley plant.

Teeling remembers: 'I couldn't lose – there were ten column stills and a fully equipped laboratory. The scrap value alone was greater than the £106,000 I paid for the entire site with fourteen acres.' In 1988, as Pernod Ricard were fighting for control of Irish Distillers, Dr John Teeling was realising a lifelong dream. He had done a deal with Lee Mallaghan to purchase the Locke's brand, and had no intention of plundering the Cooley plant – Teeling wanted to establish the first independent whiskey distillery to be formed in over a century.

While drinking in Boston's The Plough and the Stars bar in 1971, John Teeling had met Willie McCarter. Both had done case studies on Irish whiskey, John as part of his doctorate at the Harvard Business School. 'Irish Distillers was incredibly mismanaged,' remembers Teeling, 'and we felt we could do better.'

During the 1970s and 1980s, Teeling and McCarter had various business dealings, mainly in textiles, but never discussed whiskey. Teeling globetrotted, drilling for oil in Bolivia, digging for gold in Zimbabwe and manufacturing brassieres in Ireland. When, in spring 1988, news broke of Teeling's new venture, Willie McCarter was soon in contact. He had also been working on a whiskey project, having acquired the brand names and assets of the former Watt's Distillery in Derry. McCarter came on board, as did Dublin businessmen Paul Power and Donal Kinsella. With £300,000 of their own money on the line, the partners fired up

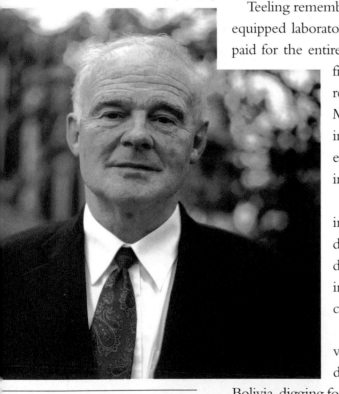

'I knew nothing about distilling, but that doesn't matter. I owned Glen Abbey which used to produce 12,500 bras a week and I never wore one, at least not in public.'

Dr John Teeling,
Chairman and Founder,
Cooley Distillery

Opposite: The Cooley Distillery in Louth, the 'wee county'.

82

the stills in Riverstown for the first time in the summer of 1989.

'I knew that Irish Distillers would say whatever I did was rubbish, so I decided to take as few chances as possible,' says Dr Teeling. 'I installed "experienced stills", used experienced distillers, traditional distillation methods, matured in single-use bourbon barrels in 200-year-old granite warehouses, and relaunched well-known brand names.' The stills from the Old Comber distillery were purchased and put to work. This was the second time the stills had been moved – prior to their time in Comber they had been used in Scotland's Ben Nevis distillery.

Like his stills, Dr Teeling's inspiration came not from Ireland, but from Scotland. The new distillery would not make triple-distilled pot still whiskey, but double-distilled malts and blends. Cooley would produce a sweet Irish whiskey similar to Scotch brands J&B and Ballantine's. These were the top sellers in the 'new' markets like France, Spain and the Far East.

'I knew it took fifty to 100 million dollars, and seven to ten years, to establish a global brand,' says Teeling. 'I also knew I didn't have that kind of money, but I did have a plan. It was a brilliant plan ... unfortunately it didn't work.'

Teeling's plan had been to sell the Locke's brand to a major player like Grand Metropolitan, Seagram or Guinness. Cooley would produce the whiskey, and leave the branding to the big boys. On 17 July 1992, as the first mature cask of Locke's Irish whiskey was being tapped by the granddaughter of John Locke, the dream of taking on Irish Distillers had turned into a nightmare. The companies that Teeling had hoped to interest had given his plan the cold shoulder. 'It went to board level with Seagrams, but in the late 'eighties no one was buying Irish except Pernod Ricard, and everyone thought they were mad. In fact they were very smart, which is why they are now taking over Seagram.'

The cash-strapped Cooley quickly took advantage of the Irish government's Business Expansion Scheme (BES). The BES allowed individuals to invest up to £25,000 a year in a company, offsetting the investment against their tax bill. It was easy to raise money for whiskey this way, and before long the confident Teeling was starting to rely on BES funds. However, the State moved to limit the scheme essentially to small business, and overnight the money dried up.

Nine million pounds of taxpayers' money had now been invested in the Cooley Distillery, but the company was sitting on 3,000,000 litres (600,000 gallons) of immature spirit that couldn't be sold and there was no cash. John Teeling had no choice but to mothball the plant. Not surprisingly, the banks started to call in their loans, and the directors had to dig into their own pockets to keep the receiver out.

As John Teeling was looking to offload the company and get his investors out, Irish Distillers arrived on the scene with a £24.5 million takeover package, a price the chairman says was 'very, very good'. Irish Distillers bought £2,000,000 worth of Cooley whiskey in order to keep the company going long enough to finalise the takeover.

'John Teeling came to us struggling, they had no financial viability,' says Richard Burrows. 'Pernod Ricard had just paid a lot of money to get hold of Irish whiskey and for very little extra we could get Cooley.' Burrows made it clear that the Cooley plant was surplus to requirements – it would be closed and the brands disbanded. 'We were secure marketing our own brands, which are all triple-distilled. This was a marketing plank worth defending.'

However, Irish Distillers' proposed takeover was referred to the Competition

Right: An old advertisement for Tyrconnell Whiskey.

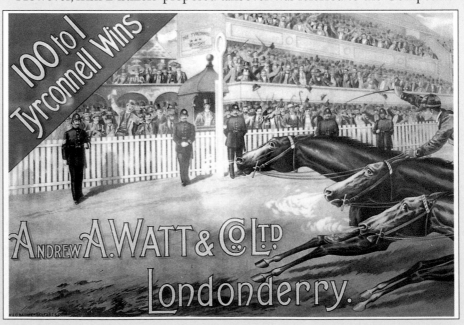

Authority, who believed that the inflated price IDL was willing to pay for Cooley proved that they were simply interested in maintaining their monopoly. On a Friday afternoon in February 1994 they rejected the takeover bid.

Teeling now had a weekend to raise the £5.8 million the banks would want come Monday morning. The American distributor Heaven Hill came on board with £1.7 million against advance sales, while Cooley's German agents Borco promised £700,000; another £1.7 million was advanced by the directors. The total of £3.4 million was enough to get the banks to back down. Cooley immediately launched The Tyrconnell single malt and the Kilbeggan blend.

The company was still far from solvent, though distilling began again on a small scale in the same year. 'We still needed £9 million to buy out the BES shareholders, as they actually owned the whiskey!' says Teeling. This was finally achieved in the year 2000. From now on, Cooley would be selling whiskey financed and owned by the company.

After a century of decline, the most moribund of drink categories has totally reinvented itself. Irish whiskey is now one of the world's most vital and exciting spirits. The fact that the Irish have just one percent of the global whiskey market is no longer a source of embarrassment, but a challenge. When you look at what has been achieved in the past ten years – with the rebirth of Irish Distillers after the Pernod-Ricard takeover, with the arrival of Cooley and with C&C International now owning the Tullamore Dew brand – who knows what another decade will bring?

WASH STILL
CONTENTS
15,920 LITRES

SPIRIT STILL
CONTENTS
LITRES

No 2
15,3

THE

ART OF WHISKEY

THE SCIENCE BEHIND THE ALCHEMY

1 . THE RAW INGREDIENTS

Irish whiskey is among the most complex drinks on earth, yet it is made from nothing more spectacular than water, barley and yeast.

Water (H$_2$O)

Spend any time in Ireland and you will soon see why it is so green. The island is simply awash with water. This is good news, as there is no point in attempting to make whiskey if you do not have a plentiful and reliable source of fresh, clean H$_2$O.

Historically, distilleries have always been sited near rivers, as water is needed for seeping, mashing, brewing, fermenting, cooling and diluting. In times past the river, more often than not, also powered all of a distillery's machines. The giant waterwheels in Kilbeggan and Midleton clearly show how essential water was to the whole production process. In fact, by the end of the nineteenth century, so many mills, breweries and distilleries were using water from Cork's River Lee, that by the time it reached the sea it was often reduced to nothing more than a trickle, and quite a polluted one at that.

Pages 86–87: Pot stills at the Old Bushmills Distillery. These pages: The Cooley water source at Slieve na gCloc, County Louth.

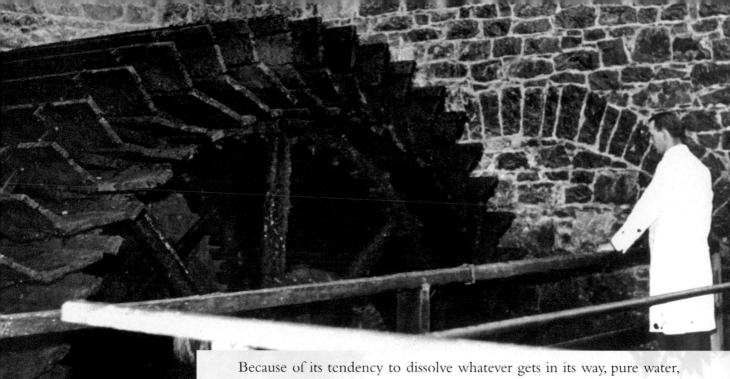

Above: The waterwheel at the Tullamore Distillery.

Because of its tendency to dissolve whatever gets in its way, pure water, in the scientific sense, rarely occurs in nature. Therefore the water used in each of Ireland's three distilleries is as different as the surrounding landscape. What effect does this have on the finished product? It is hard to say, as Ireland's three distilleries produce radically different types of whiskey. 'It's therefore hard to assess the impact of water on the completed whiskey,' says Bushmills Master Distiller Dave Quinn. 'Something like the shape of the still neck is much easier to quantify.'

The water that streams past, and indeed under, the Old Bushmills Distillery is relatively hard, with a high mineral content. This is derived from the volcanic basalt rock that it flows over, the same rock that makes up County Antrim's famous Giant's Causeway.

At the far end of the country, the source of the water used in Midleton is, and has always been, the slowly meandering Dungourney River. The water used in the making of Jameson, Paddy and Powers is therefore as soft as the leafy East Cork countryside.

'If you put rubbish in, you get rubbish out,' as Noel Sweeney of Cooley Distillery succinctly puts it. 'Obviously water is crucial, you need a good, fresh supply and you don't just need quality – you also need quantity.' Which is why, halfway up Slieve na gCloc, twinkling in the late summer sun, is a small reservoir – the carefully guarded Cooley source. Here several underground springs are dammed and the water is piped downhill to two further reservoirs. 'You don't want to run dry at just the wrong time,' says Noel. The water is naturally soft, and gentle sand filtering is all that is needed to purify it, though quality is, of course, constantly monitored.

Barley (*Hordeum polystichium*)

In times past, Irish whiskey was made from an eclectic mix of local grains, including wheat, rye and oats. Even potatoes and molasses were pressed into use in the 1800s when times were bad or prices were high, but the spirit thus produced was not whiskey.

Today barley is the grain of choice, as it contributes a lot of flavour and, unlike oats, doesn't turn into a thick porridge, which can stick to the bottom of the pot still and burn. Wheat is still sometimes used in Midleton.

Traditionally, distilling was a seasonal activity, beginning in late autumn when the rivers that powered distilleries were swollen, and grain stores heaved with the recently harvested spring barley. As the distilling season extended to cover most of the year, so strains of winter barley were slowly introduced. Today these account for around half of Midleton's barley needs.

The Midleton Distillery is unique in that it uses both malted and unmalted barley in its cereal mix. Neither of Ireland's other distilleries use unmalted grain. Master Distiller Barry Crockett sources all of Midleton's barley locally, from Kinsale in County Cork and Cappoquin in County Waterford. The distillery gets most of its malt from the Malting Company of Ireland.

Below: A field of barley near Kinsale, County Cork, destined for the Midleton Distillery.

Unlike Ireland's other two distilleries, Cooley uses 'peated' malt – malt that has been dried over a peat fire, as opposed to being dried in a closed kiln fired by natural gas. Master Distiller and Blender Noel Sweeney sources his peated malt on the open market, usually from either Ireland or Scotland.

Until the early 1970s, Old Bushmills used to malt its own barley. However, the small amounts used by the distillery made the practice too expensive and the maltings were closed. Today the distillery's needs are met by the Malting Company of Ireland and Minch Malt in County Kildare.

Yeast (Saccharomyces)

Yeast is a living organism and it is in the air you're breathing right now. Its life is spent propagating, eating sugar and creating by-products, and it is the by-products that interest us. 'Yeast is not hugely important for the taste profile of the finished drink,' says Noel Sweeney. 'What is more important is how efficiently it produces the enzymes that break down sugar molecules.'

'Yeast propagates on the sugar in the wort. The main by-products of this are alcohol, CO_2 and heat,' explains Barry Crockett. 'But many other compounds are generated in small amounts, including acids, esters and alcohols.' The amount and variety of these components is what makes one variety of yeast more desirable than another. 'Different yeast strains generate different combinations of these compounds,' he says. 'They in turn vary the flavour of the wash produced.'

'Yeast certainly has some impact on flavour', says Dave Quinn of Old Bushmills. 'It forms the base character in the beer. But how you ultimately deal with that in the still house is what determines the character of the final whiskey.'

2. TYPES OF WHISKEY

To earn the title of Irish whiskey, a spirit must be produced on the island of Ireland, be distilled from grain and be matured for no less than three years in oak casks. Irish whiskey cannot be sold at anything less than 40% alcohol by volume (abv).

Today three types of whiskey are produced in Ireland:

Above: Pure pot still whiskey being sampled in the warehouses of the Tullamore Distillery in the 1940s. Below: Redbreast, a pure pot still whiskey.

Pot Still Whiskey

The legal and the traditional definitions of 'pot still whiskey' are at odds with each other. Traditionally, 'pot still' referred to whiskey made from a mixture of malted and unmalted barley and other native grains. However, under Irish law, pot still whiskey is whiskey that is distilled in a pot still. In other words, any whiskey made in a pot still is entitled to claim the title; it is not necessary to use unmalted barley in the grain mix. Cooley can therefore legally label their single malts as 'pure pot still whiskey'.

93

On his travels, Alfred Barnard clearly makes a point of differentiating between 'old pot still whisky, designated Irish, and pure malt whisky'. So, for the sake of clarity, I will go with the traditional definitions used within the industry and reserve the 'pot still' designation for Irish whiskeys made from barley and malted barley in pot stills.

Today, traditional pot still whiskey, a full-bodied and flavoursome spirit, is produced only in Midleton. However, present-day brands such as Redbreast are considerably lighter and less oily than in times past. This is partly due to the fact that other grains like oats and rye that were traditionally used have been removed from the mash bill. The 'cut', or portion retained, from the final distillation has also been narrowed.

Malt Whiskey

Malt whiskey is made purely from malted barley. It is not unique to Scotland, though the Scots would like the world to believe that it is theirs alone. Malt whiskey has a different flavour profile to pot still whiskey, and can be given a smoky taste by drying the malted barley over peat fires.

Cooley and Bushmills produce most of Ireland's malt whiskey. Only small quantities are made in Midleton, and these are usually kept for blending purposes.

A 'single malt' is simply a malt whiskey from a single distillery. A 'double malt' is something you order at the bar.

Grain Whiskey

Above: Bushmills 10-year-old, a single malt whiskey. Right: Greenore, Ireland's only single grain whiskey.

Grain whiskey is produced by continuous distillation, and is usually made from maize. It is lighter in flavour than either malt or pot still whiskey. This is partly because maize is less flavoursome than barley, but mostly to do with the action of the patent still, which produces a less flavoured but more alcoholic spirit.

In Midleton, while grain whiskey is made by continuous distillation, they do not use a patent or Coffey still as is the practise at Cooley. The Coffey still produces a double-distilled grain whiskey, using an analyser and a rectifier. Irish Distillers use a three-stage distillation system, making their grain whiskey triple-distilled.

3. HOW WHISKEY IS MADE

Malting

To malt it, barley is steeped in water and then drained, to trick the seed into germinating. Germination is the process whereby the plant produces shoots, and this is when enzymes are produced which will convert the starch in the seed into sugar. At some stage this germination must be stopped, otherwise the shoots will continue to grow, using up the sugars that are needed to make whiskey. Drying the malted barley, or 'green malt', with hot air does this. If peat fires are used you will taste it in the whiskey; if heated air is used you won't. No one knows for sure when the Irish tradition of drying barley in a closed kiln, away from any peat reek, first started, but when Barnard visited these shores it was the industry practice.

Pot still whiskey is made from a mixture of malted and unmalted barley. The proportions change depending on what type of pot still whiskey is being produced. Both malt whiskey and pot still whiskey are made in batches in traditional copper pot stills. Grain whiskey is made in a

Above: The type of grain used depends on the type of whiskey being made, but either way malted barley is needed. This malted barley is from the Midleton Distillery.

continuous or column still, from a mix of around ninety-four percent maize
and six percent malted barley. Maize has a hard outer shell, so it must first
be cooked, before a small amount of malt is added to release the enzymes
necessary for converting the starch to sugar. This is then converted to
alcohol by the yeast during fermentation.

Mashing

The green malt (or a mixture of green malt and unmalted barley or maize,
depending on the type of whiskey being produced) is ground into a coarse
flour called 'grist', and dumped into a large tub known as a 'mash tun' or
'kieve'. Hot water is added and the mixture is agitated to encourage the
starch in the grain to turn into sugar.

This process is repeated three times, with the water, or 'wort', being
drained off after each mashing. The final wash is held and used in the first
mashing of the next batch of grist, ensuring a certain continuity between
batches. The spent grains, or 'draff', are then sold as animal feed.

Fermenting

The sweet water drained from the mash tun is called 'wort', and this is now pumped into the 'fermenters' or 'washbacks'. In the past these were made from wood, and the original wooden washbacks can still be seen at the Kilbeggan distillery. Today stainless-steel fermenters have replaced wooden washbacks in all of Ireland's working distilleries. Although less romantic than their wooden forefathers, stainless-steel fermenters are more hygienic and easier to clean.

Yeast is now added to the wash and fermentation begins. The warm, murky mixture starts to bubble and froth. When the wash settles down, fermentation is complete and the yeasty-smelling beer is around 9% alcohol by volume.

Distilling

Now comes the fun bit. Distilling takes place in either a traditional pot still, which looks like a large copper onion, or in a continuous still, which looks like part of an oil refinery. Whatever form of still is being used, the principle is the same: when the wort, essentially unhopped beer, is boiled, the alcohol vaporises at a lower temperature than water, so that the first vapours to rise will be alcohol. These are cooled, collected and re-distilled a second time in

Below: Beneath Midleton's pot stills lie the distillery's spirit receivers. The vast network of interconnected pipes and tanks give some idea of the complexity of the distilling process at the County Cork plant.

the case of Cooley and a second and third time in both Midleton and Bushmills. In the first distillation almost the entire 'run' is collected for re-distillation. In the subsequent distillations a much smaller portion, or 'cut', is taken.

The science, then, is simple; the art comes in choosing which part of the final run to retain and which to reject. Just as alcohol vaporises before water, so different alcohols and flavour elements come across at different times and different temperatures. Lower or simpler alcohols come across first. These 'foreshots' are pungent and unpalatable, and are returned to be re-distilled. Then comes the first of the good stuff, which is channelled into a 'spirits receiver'. One day this will be whiskey, so from now on the Customs and Excise authorities are watching.

As the run progresses, so the chemical make-up of the spirit changes, and heavier, long-chain alcohols start to come across. Finally heavy, oily 'feints' appear. Some of these alcohols are desirable; some most definitely are not. Where the cut is ended is therefore central to the final taste of the whiskey.

The spirits receiver is now full of 'new make spirit', which varies in strength depending on the number of times it has been distilled. At Bushmills, where they practise triple-distillation, they distil their new make malt spirit at 80–85% abv, while at Cooley their double-distilled malt is put into the cask at 68% abv. But neither of these spirits can be called Irish whiskey until it has been matured in wood for at least three years.

Maturing

Below: An illustration of the effects of maturation, showing just how thirsty the angels can be.

Most of the barrels in which Irish whiskey matures will previously have held bourbon or sherry, though some rum and cognac casks, port pipes and even virgin wood is used.

In the first year, the cask soaks up three percent of the new make spirit; while every year two percent of the contents will evaporate through the porous wood. Walk into any whiskey warehouse and you will smell it in the air. About four million bottles of Irish float skyward annually. This is called the 'angels' share'.

NEWWHISKEY

2 YEAR OLD WHISKEY
(7 % LOSS)

5 YEAR OLD WHISKEY
(13 % LOSS)

10 YEAR OLD WHISKEY
(23 % LOSS)

Vatting

Almost every whiskey bottling is a marriage of numerous casks, and brands like Jameson or Kilbeggan are blended to a formula. The casks to be used in the creation of a particular brand are first vatted together in giant holding tanks.

Next, the whiskey is reduced in strength, using demincralised water. It is important that any calcium present in the water is removed – if it isn't, it reacts with the wood extracts in the whiskey to produce flaky deposits of calcium oxide.

A minute amount of caramel (around .05%) may be added at this point. This is because not all casks are the same, and they don't all impart the same amount of colour. The age of the wood, the number of times it has been reused and the length of maturation are all variables that can affect the final colour of the whiskey. However, the addition of caramel does not sweeten the whiskey or affect the taste in any way.

Just prior to bottling, the whiskey is chill-filtered – that is, cooled to between zero and four degrees Celsius and filtered. This removes deposits dissolved in the alcohol which may turn the whiskey cloudy when water or ice is added. Like the addition of caramel, this exercise has little or no effect on flavour, provided the filtration temperature doesn't go below zero degrees.

Above: Casks being filled with 'new make spirit' at Cooley's Kilbeggan warehouses.

Above: A fire in the North Mall Distillery closed the plant in 1920. However, the buildings currently house two bottling lines, where, among other brands, Jameson is still bottled.

Bottling

The final stage of the process is bottling. Bushmills bottle their own whiskey on site, while Cooley ship their mature stocks by road from Kilbeggan back to the County Louth distillery for bottling. Most whiskey from Midleton is bottled at a large bottling plant outside Dublin, but by far the most interesting plant in the country is to be found in Cork City. Although silent since a fire in 1920, the North Mall Distillery is now home to two small bottling lines. Here modern stainless steel and old crumbling stone live side-by-side, in the country's most overlooked piece of distilling history.

Above: Cooley's Master Distiller
Noel Sweeney inspects the pot stills
during their yearly spring-clean.

4. THE FLAVOUR ELEMENTS

Distillation

Spend any time discussing whiskey with either Dave Quinn or Noel
Sweeney, and the conversation will always come back to the same topic:
distillation. Barry Crockett, whose father before him was also a master
distiller, talks about the subject with equal passion.

The reason is simple: in Ireland all whiskeys have to be distilled in-house.
By contrast, most bottles of Scotch contain whiskies sourced from a variety
of different distilleries, companies and regions. These malt and grain whiskies
are then blended to create well-known brands like Johnnie Walker or
Teacher's. If one of the constituent whiskies cannot be sourced from its usual
supplier, it can be replaced.

The Irish Distillers plants at Midleton and Bushmills have to provide all
of the whiskeys for the Group's numerous brands. Bushmills make just one
type of malt whiskey, while the complex Midleton plant produces a range
of separate whiskey types. If whiskey of a certain age or wood finish runs

Above: One of the mighty stills from John Power & Sons now sits outside the old distillery, Midleton.

out, another similar one cannot be conjured out of thin air or bought on the open market. Likewise the three types of whiskey produced by Cooley, one grain and two malts, when matured in different woods, make up the total inventory that goes into the company's portfolio of brands. Arguably, this puts distillation at the core of what makes Irish whiskey unique.

Twice or Thrice?

Like many bits of received wisdom, the 'fact' that Irish whiskey is and always has been triple-distilled more than stretches the truth.

From Barnard's accounts, it is not always clear which Irish distilleries operated a system of triple-distillation and which did not. All of the Dublin distillers certainly did, but at Monasterevin, on his first trip into rural Ireland, Barnard wrote the following: 'From the receiver, the pure spirit, which has undergone two distillations, is pumped into the three spirit vats, placed in the spirit store, where we followed it.'

Certainly eight of the twenty-eight Irish distilleries he visited practised double-distillation, including Old Bushmills. Here Barnard described how, 'we were conducted to the still house, a very large building, containing two old fashioned pot stills, holding 2,500 and 1,500 gallons each.'

With the collapse of the industry in the 1920s, double-distilled Irish passed into history and for a time, until the arrival of Cooley, all Irish whiskey was indeed triple-distilled.

Cooley's insistence on double-distillation vexed Irish Distillers no end. One of their key selling points, that Irish was 'smoother' than Scotch because it was triple-distilled, was no longer a universal truth. As we have seen, this, along with the County Louth distillery's use of peated malt, was a factor driving the attempted Irish Distillers takeover of Cooley. 'It is one of the issues we were concerned about,' Richard Burrows said at the time. To this day, the issue remains divisive.

'The real issue isn't the number of stills you have, but rather the still design.' So says Cooley Managing Director David Hynes. 'Both of our stills are the same size and have wide necks which gives us lots of partial condensation and reflux. When we ran them it worked; there was no need to distil a third time.'

Not surprisingly, Dave Quinn takes a different approach. 'Triple-distillation makes a huge difference, it gives a different style of whiskey.' The Old Bushmills Master Distiller is almost evangelical on the joys of a third still. 'I'm often asked, what does the third distillation do?' he continues. 'I'll tell you. It pushes out the flavour spectrum and gives you a lighter, more fragrant, fruity, floral, spicy character. You leave the higher alcohols and fusel oils behind, so removing the heaviness.'

'Which is better?' muses Cooley's Noel Sweeney. 'You can argue the thing to suit yourself. A more refined whiskey could also be called a blander whiskey. What we do suits us, what Irish Distillers do suits them.'

To Barry Crockett of Midleton, the science speaks for itself. 'If you have two distillations you get a greater range of compounds retained. There's a certain pungency from double-distilled whiskey. There's nothing wrong with that – it's just not what we do.'

Below: Noel Sweeney, Cooley Master Distiller and Blender, close to the distillery's water source.
Bottom: Dave Quinn, Old Bushmills Master Distiller, in his local pub in the town of Bushmills.

103

Above: Hand-cutting turf in the
traditional manner with a *sleán*.

Peat

Ireland is shaped like a saucer, with mountains around the edge and a huge
dip in the middle. This dip is dotted with lakes, alive with rivers and damp
with bogs. Here fallen vegetation that has been unable to rot due to
waterlogging, has been compressed by yet more sodden vegetation and
slowly turned into dark brown turf or peat.

For centuries peat, cut in the summer and dried in the sun, heated Irish
homes, while food was cooked over the turf fire in an all-purpose cooking
pot called a bastible. In a country with precious few other natural resources,
peat was free and it was most plentiful in the poorest of counties,
traditionally home to the *poitín* maker.

Peat once played a much more important role in the manufacture and
taste of Irish whiskey than it does today. Barley would be soaked in bog
water, while slowly burning peat flavoured the malt and gave an even heat
to the stills. It is therefore very probable that in the past Irish whiskey was
pretty heavily peated.

Today most of the barley for Irish whiskey is dried in closed kilns, keeping the smoke at bay, and steam jets heat modern pot stills. Just as no one knows when triple-distillation became the common Irish practice, so no one knows when Irish distilleries switched to closed kilns. 'In a country full of bogs, why peated malt never caught on is a real mystery,' says Dave Quinn of Old Bushmills. 'But I guess it was tried and just didn't sell as well.'

Today Cooley produce Ireland's only peated whiskeys. Ironically, they are matured in Kilbeggan where, in the 1940s, the cash-strapped Locke's resorted to using local turf to fire their stills when imported coal became too expensive.

Copper

Because of its many desirable properties, such as its resistance to corrosion, its malleability and its lustrous beauty, copper is one of the most widely used elements, and was probably the first metal from which useful articles were made by man.

However, copper is also the Cinderella of the whiskey world, ignored by writers, who prefer to wax lyrical about tumbling waterfalls, and taken for granted by all but those in the know. The truth is that copper plays a huge role in shaping the flavour of Irish whiskey, so much so that even modern, stainless-steel continuous stills have copper heads.

Below: The original pot stills from Locke's Distillery were sold for scrap a week before the price of copper fell through the floor. These stills in Kilbeggan are actually from the neighbouring Tullamore Distillery and have gone green with age and neglect. A little TLC, however, is all that is needed to restore their colour. Restoring them to life will be a much bigger job.

Walk into any Irish distillery and you will see massive copper pot stills reaching proudly for the sky. The element plays an essential role in the alchemy of distilling, for the copper in the stills reacts with the spirit being produced, neutralising bad components and giving a piece of itself up to every distillation. Over a period of decades the stills wear thin, until they have to be replaced. When this happens, distillers make sure that the replacements are as close to the originals as possible.

The distillation process isn't very selective – along with the good stuff comes bad stuff. 'What copper does is help remove the bad guys,' says Dave Quinn. 'Copper's main work is in removing undesirable sulphur compounds.'

'It does this by reacting with the sulphur to produce copper sulphate, which is subsequently filtered out,' says Midleton's Barry Crockett. 'This is why stainless-steel stills don't work, and column stills must have copper heads.'

Wood

Of all the elements that come together to produce the flavour of Irish whiskey, wood is easily the most significant, yet it is the most recent. Early whiskey was never allowed to age, but was drunk straight from the still. In fact, it wasn't until 1915 that the ageing of whiskey in wooden barrels was made mandatory. This, more than anything else, has the most profound effect on the taste of the modern drink.

'Maturation has a huge influence,' says Dave Quinn. 'I'd say fifty percent of the final flavour comes from the wood. Something like mouthfeel is all down to the interaction of the spirit and wood.'

In all likelihood, whiskey was first stored in wooden casks in the 1700s, when the trade started using barrels for the transport of whiskey. Along the way some happy merchant probably discovered that whiskey that had been in a cask for a time mellowed nicely.

Irish whiskey is usually matured in casks that have held a previous alcoholic beverage. This isn't because distillers are too mean to buy new barrels, but rather because new wood is very assertive and can easily overpower a whiskey. Distilleries in Ireland and Scotland have always used seasoned casks.

Today Brendan Monks has special responsibility for securing all of the wood used by Irish Distillers. He has very specific requirements, and travels the world sourcing and maintaining the company's vast wood portfolio. Distilleries haven't always been so particular.

'In the past, distillers and merchants used whatever casks were to hand,' he explains. 'Traditionally they would have had access to oloroso, port, Madeira, Malaga and other fortified wines that today are obscure, but back in the nineteenth century were as well known as sherry.' These wines would have been imported into Ireland still in their casks, which, when emptied, were filled with whiskey.

While most of today's Irish whiskey is matured in barrels that have previously held bourbon, in times past Irish whiskey was subject to an eclectic variety of wood types. Recent developments at Bushmills, where whiskey was finished in port and Madeira wood, are therefore nothing more than the re-establishment of an age-old tradition.

Above: One of the maturation warehouses in the Midleton complex.

The Process

Marketing departments like to sell the image of barrels slumbering in silent, dark warehouses – a static, inactive process. The truth, however, is much more interesting. Whiskey casks don't just sit there gathering dust; inside, complex chemical reactions are taking place. Changes that turn fiery new make spirit into mellow Irish whiskey; a transformation that, for all our scientific knowledge, we still don't completely understand.

In the same way that mercury in a thermometer expands and contracts when heated and cooled, so throughout the natural temperature cycle of the seasons, the maturing spirit expands and contracts. As it warms and expands, the whiskey pushes into the porous wood and some of it evaporates through the staves. In the winter, when the air temperature drops, the alcohol contracts, creating a vacuum in the cask and drawing in oxygen and leached extracts from the wood, which then interact with the maturing spirit. 'The cask is breathing like a lung,' says Monks.

It is a complicated chemical reaction, which results in a purification of the ageing spirit. Brendan Monks puts it a lot more poetically. 'Maturation in wood can be described as a fourth distillation, in that over time the spirit is further purified. That's the magic that takes place in the cask.'

Today Irish whiskey is mainly matured in two types of cask, bourbon barrels and sherry butts. The former are usually made from American white oak *(Quercus alba)*, and the latter from European oak *(Quercus robur)*.

American Oak: Due to the modern practice of bottling sherry and other fortified wines at the vineyard prior to export, the supply of casks that have contained fortified wines has disappeared. At the same time, a huge growth in the bourbon industry and the falling price of transatlantic transport have made American wood a real alternative. Ex-bourbon casks also have a more subtle effect on the whiskey than sherry, which can easily swamp the lighter shape of modern whiskey.

By United States law, bourbon has to be matured in new wood. This more aggressive spirit needs, and can take, the heavy doses of vanilla-type flavour that come from fresh oak. Happily, this ensures a constant supply of second-hand barrels.

Prior to their first use in America, new barrels are charred. 'This opens the grains of the oak, to allow greater ingress of the spirit,' says Brendan Monks. It also produces a layer of carbon, which will later help to remove unwanted flavour compounds from maturing Irish whiskey.

New American oak barrels are not widely used to mature Irish. Recently, however, Midleton Master Blender Barry Walsh has been using small amounts of whiskey matured in virgin wood, for example in Jameson Gold.

Cooley matures its whiskey almost exclusively in bourbon wood, from the Heaven Hill distillery in Kentucky. Irish Distillers source their American oak from their sister distillery Wild Turkey, which is also part of the Pernod Ricard group. Brendan Monks also gets additional barrels from Jack Daniels, Makers Mark and Jim Beam. In fact he spends so much type in Tennessee, he has picked up the nickname Colonel Monks.

Below: American oak barrels are charred in Kentucky prior to being sent to the Heaven Hill Distillery to be filled with bourbon. Once emptied, these casks will be shipped to Ireland where they will give a good home to Cooley's whiskey.

European oak: Unlike American barrels, which can be bought on the open market, fortified-wine casks for Irish Distillers have to be specially commissioned. Whether it be sherry butts or port pipes, this is a long, slow and expensive process, and every stage has to be personally overseen by Brendan Monks.

The timber is first logged, cut into 'stave' and 'heading' wood and then air-dried for up to two years. The casks are then assembled and seasoned with a specially selected fortified wine such as oloroso sherry. Unlike bourbon wood, these casks are not charred on the inner staves.

The casks then sit in Jerez in Spain, or Oporto in Portugal, for two-and-a-half to three years, with Irish Distillers paying for the privilege, before the contents are emptied and the casks are shipped to Ireland.

Lifespan

'Wood is so important in making up the flavour profile of a whiskey,' says Noel Sweeney, who uses a combination of first-, second- and third-fill bourbon barrels to mature the majority of Cooley's whiskeys. Each filling leaches more and more from the wood, so after the third outing, the only thing a bourbon cask is good for is growing strawberries in.

Brendan Monks also retires his bourbon wood after its third outing. Expensive sherry casks get used just twice, while casks from rum, port and other fortified wines are retired after just one filling. Most casks are either sent to garden centres or sold on to Scottish distilleries. Here they are often re-charred or impregnated with paxarete, a sherry-like syrup, and put back into use. This dubious practice is not carried out by any Irish distillery.

Opposite: Oloroso sherry butts destined for Ireland must first spend up to three years in a Spanish bodega. Below: On the edge of the Brusna River, Kilbeggan, dead barrels await a truck to take them to a garden centre near you.

Time

The final and most elusive of the flavour elements is maturation. While the quality of yeast, water, barley and even barrels may vary, time is the one constant.

To be entitled to the name 'Irish whiskey', spirit must be matured in wood for a minimum of three years. The age stated on a bottle is that of the youngest whiskey used in that particular bottling. For example, Jameson 1780 is labelled as a twelve-year-old; this means that the youngest cask of whiskey used was twelve years old, though other casks could well have been older.

The surface-to-volume ratio of a cask is an important factor in maturation. A bourbon barrel is smaller than a sherry butt, so the former has a higher surface-to-volume ratio than the latter. This means that whiskey in the bourbon barrel will mature faster, as it has more contact with the wood and air.

We also know that maturation happens in fits and starts. Periods where the whiskey tastes pretty dull are interspersed with times when it is ripe, followed by more dullness, until the flavours fall into line and the whiskey works again.

Climate, too, plays an important part in maturation. As a general rule of thumb, the warmer the weather, the faster the spirit will age. Whiskey therefore matures more slowly in Scotland than in Ireland, which sits mild and damp in the Gulf Stream. This warm current flows from the Straits of Florida and helps keep Irish winters milder, and Irish summers cooler, than other places on the same latitude. Even on the island there are variations – Barry Crockett of Midleton reckons that whiskey matures more quickly in County Cork than in County Antrim.

5.BLENDING

'Distilling is a science and blending is an art.' So says Sam Bronfman, founder of multinational drinks company Seagram. While the art of blending is often overlooked, the fact is that Ireland's best-selling whiskeys are all blends.

Any skilled artist makes what he does seem easy, and, watching Barry Walsh and Noel Sweeney at work, what master blenders do looks deceptively simple. Of course it is anything but – anyone can pick up a brush, but true artists are few and far between. So when it comes to whiskey, where does the art come in?

'The art is in creating a new and complex taste experience that is greater than the sum of the individual components of the blend,' says Barry Walsh, filling a row of glasses. Noel Sweeney agrees: 'You sit down with some bottles and mix up what you think is going to work, but to do that you really have to know how your raw materials will go together.' These 'raw materials', or 'building blocks' as Barry Walsh calls them, are the various whiskeys produced, whether by Cooley or by Irish Distillers.

Above: A line of nosing glasses await the attention of Master Blender Noel Sweeney, at the Cooley Distillery, County Louth.

Starting from Scratch

Most of a blender's time is spent not in creating new whiskeys, but rather in maintaining the flavour profile of existing brands. Jameson, Tullamore Dew and Black Bush, for example, are all produced to a formula of whiskey types and cask types, with a particular age profile. But there is no doubt that creating a new blend is the glamorous and exciting bit, so let's begin there.

'It starts with a brief from marketing,' says Barry Walsh. 'For example, take the case of Jameson Gold: they wanted a premium blend in the Jameson camp. We had some whiskey maturing in virgin new wood on a trial basis and, as it turned out, this whiskey became the key to the blend.'

Above: Irish Distillers Master Blender Barry Walsh at work in his Dublin laboratory.

However, premium blends must feature a range of older whiskeys, and these cannot be conjured out of thin air. With very old whiskeys in fairly short supply, it was decided not to feature an age statement. This gave Barry Walsh greater latitude in pulling together the whiskeys – eventually ranging in age from eight to twenty years – needed to make the blend work.

After blending two or three different profiles, a formulation for Jameson Gold was agreed. Barry Walsh had to be sure that this was sustainable. Part of the job is to ensure that the whiskeys that make up a brand are always available in sufficient quantities to meet sales forecasts. The whiskeys, when they come forward for blending, must also conform to their normal taste profile; that is, they must taste much the same as they always have done.

'It's a logistical nightmare,' says Cooley's Noel Sweeney. 'Locke's Malt, for example, carries an eight-year age statement. So I have to have enough whiskey to sustain sales of that brand over eight years, because that is how long it will take to replenish stock.'

Although single malts, like Locke's or Bushmills, or pure pot still whiskeys, like Redbreast, are not blends, they are still the result of the vatting together of numerous casks. Two identical casks filled with the same distillate can produce radically different results. 'I just nosed forty-eight casks this morning,' says Noel Sweeney, 'and three of them were very different to all the others.' These casks will be put aside. Some may contain whiskey that will mature into liquid gold.

Having a good nose, then, is only part of the job. Blenders also have to be part accountant and part soothsayer. 'There is a lot of planning and routine checking involved in the blender's day-to-day function,' Barry Walsh concludes. 'It's not very romantic, but it is very necessary.'

6. TASTING IRISH WHISKEY

The Science of Taste

Pour yourself a glass of any Irish whiskey. It contains forty percent pure and clear ethyl alcohol, and almost sixty percent tasteless water. The 'almost' is very important, however, for without it you would be drinking vodka, and you clearly are not. The spirit in your glass is not clear – it is a nutty amber colour; if you swish it around, it smells of all kinds of wonderful things that you can't quite put a name to; also, unlike vodka, it tastes of something.

What you are experiencing here are the 'congeners' – the flavour elements, which in any decent whiskey only account for between 0.1% and 0.2% of what is in your glass. Put it this way: if you were throwing a party and your bath was full of alcohol and water, then the flavour elements you would need to turn it magically into whiskey would fit into an eggcup.

Congeners are simply the aromas and flavours produced during the making of spirits. Professional 'noses' have been able to identify 350 separate

Above: The taste of a whiskey owes a lot to the maturation process. The effect that time and wood have on clear new make spirit is evident in these five bottles. From left to right: whiskey matured for three years in third-fill bourbon wood, second-fill bourbon wood and first-fill bourbon wood. The last two show the effects of, respectively, second-fill and first-fill sherry casks.

and individual congeners in whiskey. But there are well over a thousand, many of which are still unidentified. Some have come from the barley, some from the distillation process itself and some from maturation.

In an attempt to isolate the elements of taste that come from distillation, scientists in Irish Distillers can recreate the distillation process in the laboratory and isolate various fractions, or portions, which have differing tastes. These fractions can then be put through a gas chromatographic column which separates out in sequence the lightest and the heaviest congeners. These congeners, or flavours, can be timed and nosed as they emerge sequentially from the end of the column. This allows Barry Walsh to nose the entire distillation process in real time.

A Tasting

Pubs are great places to drink whiskey, but they are terrible places to taste the stuff. The air is too full of other smells — beer, floor polish, smoke and that guy in the corner eating crisps.

Professional tastings take place in a sterile environment. No one wears perfume or deodorant; the glasses are rinsed to remove any soap deposits and left to drip-dry, lest they be tainted by a grubby tea-towel. In the laboratories of Irish Distillers, for example, the use of Dettol and similar disinfectants is banned. 'They ruin your nose,' explains Master Blender

Below: My local, in downtown Clonakilty.

Barry Walsh, sniffing the air. Perhaps someone has forgotten to tell one of the cleaners, as Barry rushes off to have a quiet word.

You don't have to take it to this extreme, but if you are serious about it, it is best to taste whiskeys in a bright room where there are no strong odours.

You will need

1. A bottle of Irish whiskey, or, better still, grab a couple of bottles for comparison tasting.

2. A jug and a glass of spring water. Tap water will do if you let it stand for half an hour or so, to allow any chlorine that may be present to disperse. The jug is for diluting, the glass for refreshing the palate.

3. A glass or glasses for your whiskey. Forget tumblers – they were designed by the Americans for whiskey and soda, and are utterly useless for the job in hand. Professional tasters use a whiskey-nosing glass, but a sherry or, at a pinch, a wine glass will do. What you are looking for is a glass with a bowl to cradle and warm the whiskey in your hand, and tall, tapering sides to retain the aroma of the spirit.

Since we are in this for pleasure, let's take the sensual rather than the analytic approach. We have to feed our senses:

Sound

Break the seal, pop that cork and pour. As the whiskey falls into the glass, you will hear the sound James Joyce described as 'light music'. Joyce was so proud of sharing initials with John Jameson that he had his wallet engraved 'JJ', using the same typeface as the Bow Street distiller.

Sight

Forget about taste for a moment, and let's have a little foreplay: hold your glass up to the light. What can your eyes tell you about a whiskey? A huge amount actually, which is why in 'blind tastings', where the whiskeys being tasted are anonymous, cobalt-blue glasses are used, lest the colour give anything away.

For a start, your eyes can tell you the strength of the drink. Swirl the spirit around in the glass and look at its 'legs'. These are the long trails left by the whiskey as it slips down the side of the glass. The longer the legs, the higher the alcoholic content.

Now, look carefully at the spirit, as not all whiskey is the same colour. Is the whiskey pale straw (Connemara), or amber (Jameson 1780), or is it tinged with ruby (Bushmills 16 year-old malt)? Colour can tell you a lot about the wood in which the whiskey was matured. A pale colour suggests bourbon wood, and indeed Connemara is matured exclusively in ex-bourbon casks. Darker whiskey like Jameson 1780 could be showing the effects of part-maturation in sherry butts. In the case of Bushmills sixteen-year-old malt, that ruby glow comes from the port pipes which lend this whiskey its special character.

Smell

The nose is a very delicate instrument, and one of the most advanced and overlooked organs in the body. It is capable of detecting odours diluted to one part in a million; while there are only four primary tastes, there are thirty-two primary smells.

The nose also plays a large part in detecting flavours, which is why when your nose is blocked most foods taste bland. More often than not, when we talk about 'taste', we are largely talking about smell.

When you breathe in, air is rushed to the olfactory bulb, which sits at the back of the nostrils. From here, signals are transmitted to an area in the cerebral cortex called the hypothalamus, which, besides dealing with smell, handles emotional and sexual responses. The nose, then, is hardwired directly to the most primitive part of the brain, and this is why smells can be very evocative, even emotional.

Start by getting the 'nose-feel' for the whiskey. This is the prickle you get when you swirl the whiskey around in your glass and sniff. That tingle is alcohol; sniff again and it will anaesthetise your nose and you will smell nothing. If this happens, sniff a glass of water or go outside for a moment. Your nose grows accustomed to smells – after a while a person can become used to just about any aroma. So it is important not to sniff too hard or too often – simply note your initial impressions and move on.

Now dilute the whiskey, and watch as eddies of water release the bouquet. Professional tasters nose at 20% abv – half whiskey, half water – but they also spit the stuff out. Do whatever feels best, but do add at least a drop of H_2O and your nose will be richly rewarded.

With the addition of water, many of the keynotes you noted earlier will be more prevalent, but beware the noisy ones – peat, vanilla and sherry are first out, and tend to smother other, finer aromas. Note the obvious, then move on to tasting.

Mouthfeel

As well as detecting taste, the tongue is where 'mouthfeel' – the texture and smoothness of the whiskey – are experienced. What does the whiskey feel like in your mouth? Swirl it around – some, like Jameson Gold, are fat and syrupy; others, like Tullamore Dew, are light and spirity.

Taste

Now pull in some air and the whiskey will come to life. What is up first – sweetness? Peat? Vanilla? A good whiskey will set off a chain of reactions on your tongue, sparking sensations all over, sometimes all at once, sometimes in sequence.

Taste is registered by receptors – the taste buds – located on the surface and sides of the tongue. Those at the tip of the tongue transmit sweetness, whereas saltiness and sourness are transmitted from the sides.

Finally, swallow. What is the residual taste? Is it pleasant? How long does it last? This is called the 'finish'. A poor whiskey will be gone as soon as it slides down your throat; a good one will rumble on for some time.

Below: A 'ball of malt'.

Putting Words to Taste

Over the past couple of years, the industry has been playing catch-up, and now even the most modest bottle of Irish comes complete with fanciful tasting notes. However, more often than not, they are written by the marketing department and leave the drinker lost, wondering why their glass doesn't contain 'woody muscle' or 'hot cross buns'.

These word-sketches are, of course, subjective, and just because somebody working for the distillery can smell 'sherry-maltiness' doesn't mean you will – in fact, it doesn't mean it even exists. Everybody's sense of smell is different and, to complicate things further, we don't all describe the same smell the same way.

Irish Whiskey Tasting Wheel

This stylised wheel is designed to illustrate how the production and maturation processes affect the overall taste of Irish whiskey. In the centre are objective terms, and on the outer rim more subjective terms, which can be used when describing a whiskey.

Mouthfeel: Not a taste in itself but a taste attribute, this sensation is largely influenced by maturation. 'Viscous', 'thin' and 'round' are just some of the adjectives commonly used to describe this tactile experience.

Phenolic: Phenols are the hydroxyl derivatives of aromatic hydrocarbons. In other words, this term refers to the 'peaty' or 'phenolic' nose found in whiskeys where the malted barley has been dried over a peat fire.

Feinty: 'Feints' are the rather oily-tasting compounds which come over later in the distillation. Although less desirable than pure alcohols, small fractions can contribute a lot to a whiskey's character. These days, less feints are taken than in times past – this and triple-distillation mean that feinty notes in Irish whiskey are very rare.

Cereal: Barley, particularly the unmalted variety, leaves its cereal imprint on most Irish whiskeys, particularly those with a high pot still whiskey content. Grain whiskeys produced from maize in a continuous still are milder and have less cereal character.

Aldehydic: When higher alcohols come in contact with the air during distillation in the pot still, each alcohol gives rise to its own aldehyde. These chemicals are mysterious in origin, but the aldehydes created from a wash of unmalted barley give Irish pot still whiskey its signature crackle.

Estery: Distillation not only produces alcohols, but also a range of other compounds, such as acids and esters. The latter are formed by the reaction between alcohols and acids and, since any acid can react with any alcohol, it is clear that this is where the unique 'nose' of many a whiskey is actually born.
For example, amyl acetate, which is produced when amyl alcohol reacts with acetic acid, is the smell of pear drops; octyl acetate is the smell of oranges, while methyl butyrate gives you pineapples.

Winey: Compounds acquired from the previous contents of the cask, such as sherry, port or Madeira. New whiskey is clear at first. It will take all of its colour, and perhaps fifty percent of its flavour, from the cask.

Oily: Nutty or oily flavours, which usually derive from oak lactones leached out during maturation.

Wood extractives: During its time in the cask, maturing whiskey reacts with the oak. Flavour elements are added from the wood, like vanilla notes and some tannins.

Musty: Found only in very old whiskeys that have spent a long time in a damp, dark warehouse. Nowadays, whiskey warehouses are invariably large, dry, airy structures.

Now that you have read the theory, pour yourself some Irish whiskey, go back to the start of this chapter and have some fun.

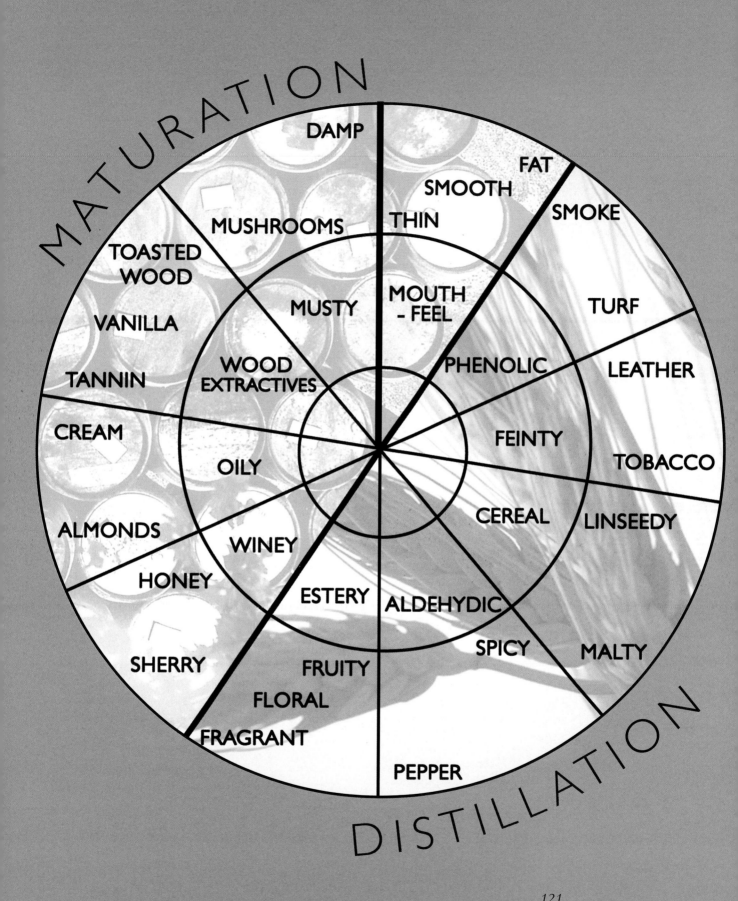

MATURATION

DISTILLATION

DAMP
MUSHROOMS
TOASTED WOOD
VANILLA
TANNIN
CREAM
ALMONDS
HONEY
SHERRY

MUSTY
WOOD EXTRACTIVES
OILY
WINEY
ESTERY
FRUITY
FLORAL
FRAGRANT

SMOOTH
THIN
FAT
MOUTH-FEEL
SMOKE
TURF
LEATHER
TOBACCO
LINSEEDY
MALTY

PHENOLIC
FEINTY
CEREAL
ALDEHYDIC
SPICY
PEPPER

AN A TO Z

OF IRISH WHISKEY

THE ULTIMATE GUIDE TO THE WATER OF LIFE

An A to Z of Irish Whiskey

The tasting notes for this book were done blind. In other words, I never knew what whiskey was lurking behind the cobalt-blue glass. This meant that my brand prejudices (and we all have them) were not allowed to taint my notes.

Also, certain words were banned. In all my years of drinking whiskey, I have yet to try a brand that didn't claim to be either 'smooth' or 'mellow', or sometimes both, when often it was neither. By now the 's' and 'm' words have been trotted out so many times that they are totally meaningless.

An important point about whiskey tasting is that we all experience the world in our own unique way. Just because one person can smell pear drops, doesn't necessarily mean that everyone will. To further complicate things, none of us will describe the same taste or sensation in exactly the same manner, which is why group tasting can be so informative and fun.

So, far from these notes being the final word on the subject, let them be just the beginning. Rather than simply drinking Irish whiskey, taste the stuff, and then please feel free to disagree with any or all of what follows. Mostly though, enjoy yourself.

Tastings

This section deals with
- labels/brands which are associated with distilleries
- other labels and blends.

All are listed in alphabetical order. Boxed text gives label history and tasting notes. Occasional individual brand histories are included as unboxed text.

Colour Coding:

All boxes containing labels are colour-coded in terms of their ownership. Labels with *blue* text and outline are owned by Irish Distillers. Those with *red* text and outline are owned by Cooley Distillery. Those with *black* text are independently owned.

Tasting notes for retailer own brand whiskeys and single cask bottlings are featured on my constantly updated website www.whiskeymaster.com

Brennan's

Noel Sweeney at the Cooley Distillery blends this whiskey exclusively for the American wholesaler Shaw-Ross.

Nose: A great full-on nose of spicy malt and gentle peat.

Taste: That signature Cooley sweetness, then soft, warm spicy tickles and milk drops.

Finish: Uncomplicated, with some firm grain giving way to distant peat.

Comments: Obviously a young grain-heavy blend, but it goes down very easily. A solid entry-level Irish.

OLD BUSHMILLS DISTILLERY

'After crossing the River Bush, we found ourselves at the old-fashioned town of Bushmills, and within a few minutes' walk of the Distillery. The company have recently increased the capacity of their old Pot Stills, and erected the electric light on their premises, which has a very pleasing effect, and shows that they are alive to all modern inventions.' Alfred Barnard, 1887

Of the twenty-eight Irish distilleries visited by Barnard, this is the only establishment where whiskey is still made.

Barnard writes: 'The first record we have of this, no doubt the oldest Distillery in Ireland, is in the year 1743, when it was in the hands of a band of smugglers; but in 1784 we find it recognised as a legitimate distillery.' In fact, in 1782 there were five licensed distilleries in Bushmills, but thereafter they all disappear, probably underground. Either way, it is 1833 before a James McKibben is recorded as paying duty on whiskey distilled in the town. Thereafter the distillery had a succession of owners.

On 28 November 1885, disaster struck when the distillery was ravaged by fire. However, these were the boom years and, before long, the entire distillery had been rebuilt from the ground up. This is why Old Bushmills bears more than a passing resemblance to many Scottish distilleries of the period.

It was around this time that Samuel Wilson Boyd first got involved with the Old Bushmills distillery; he eventually bought the distillery in 1923. Boyd was a strict Presbyterian, who wrote temperance pamphlets in his spare time. But he had a real feel for business and, under his management, the distillery prospered. Two years after his death in 1932, two of his fourteen children, Austin and Wilson Boyd, succeeded him and ran the company until the mid-1960s.

Shortly after the end of the Second World War, Isaac Wolfson, the Belfast textile magnate, started to buy his way into Old Bushmills, though the Boyd brothers remained as company directors. Under Wolfson's growing influence, Old Bushmills whiskey began to be shipped around the world.

In 1964 Wolfson sold the distillery to the English Brewers Charrington. However, distilling was of secondary importance to the beer giant; by the early 1970s Bushmills was back on the market.

As we saw in the history section, the Seagram Company of Montreal then acquired the distillery. In 1976 Seagram obtained a twenty percent holding in Irish Distillers and, as part of an agreement, the Old Bushmills Distillery soon became a wholly-owned subsidiary of the Irish Distillers Group.

Bushmills

Nicknamed 'White Bush' because of the white label, this whiskey is a roughly fifty:fifty blend of Bushmills malt, aged between six and seven years, and Midleton grain, aged four to five years.

Nose: An almost silent whisper of rose water and fortified wine.

Taste: Mouth-filling sweetness that quickly gives way to rich cocoa and a hint of fruit loaf.

Finish: The chocolate is now dark and slightly bitter. Very long and quite delicious.

Comments: This is a whiskey that has pulled its socks up in recent years. The grain, which once dominated the blend, is now held on a lead by some superb malt.

Black Bush

A whiskey with a malt content of around eighty percent, blended with grain whiskey produced at Midleton especially for the brand. At one time, the grain for Black Bush was distilled at Coleraine, where the old and rather inefficient patent still produced a mild, estery-sweet grain whiskey. When Coleraine closed and Bushmills joined Irish Distillers, the sweet grain, which worked so well in Black Bush, was replicated in Midleton. This whiskey benefits from lots of sherry wood.

Nose: A total stunner. Someone in the next room is wearing fresh nail varnish and cooking up a pot of zesty marmalade. Sherry and light perfume also appear.

Taste: A beautifully orchestrated assault on the tongue and nose. Huge, oaked sherry, soft as silk.

Finish: Not as long as in the past, but the spicy, grainy aftertaste is still first-rate.

Comments: A completely individual whiskey that is also uniquely Irish. Quite simply one of the finest blends on the planet.

Bushmills Malt 10-year-old

Launched in 1987, this is a rich and flavourful malt, with no smoky or peaty character. It is matured in bourbon and sherry wood.

Nose: Very light. Vanilla, almonds and sherry.

Taste: A very gentle mouth bath of blanched nuts, dried fruit and toasted malt.

Finish: There's fudge quality to the finish. Quite long.

Comments: Complicated enough to be interesting, but you feel that the malt is just getting into its stride. A pleasure that won't tax the wallet or the palate too much.

Bushmills Malt 12-year-old Distillery Reserve

Available only at the distillery, this is a slightly more flavourful cousin of the ten-year-old, due to its extra time in the cask.

Nose: Intensely malty and ever-so-slightly musty.

Taste: One of the sweetest Irish whiskeys I have tasted, but not cloying in any way. Like butter melting into honey on freshly toasted bread. A chorus of figs and dates arrives just in time.

Finish: Wow. The fruit theme evolves into some wonderful woody and winey notes, which echo around before being joined by a merest hint of liquorice. Very long.

Comments: It is clear that the quality of the wood here is exceptional, and it is doubtful that a whiskey of this calibre could be produced in anything but small quantities. So you will just have to visit the distillery and buy a couple or three bottles.

Bushmills Malt 'Three Wood', 16-year-old

Bourbon- and sherry-wood matured single malt whiskeys are vatted together in port pipes for one year to produce this sixteen-year-old expression.

Nose: An exquisite belt of exotic spices, cut with rich cigar smoke.

Taste: A rich start sets off tangerines, cocoa and spicy port notes. This whiskey keeps unfolding as you hold it in the mouth. Later, nutty toffee and cocoa arrive.

Finish: The port really makes itself felt here. Very dry, yet sweet. Hints of bitter chocolate.

Comments: A hugely complex whiskey; words really cannot do it justice. This expression also marks a welcome return to the Irish tradition of maturing fine whiskey in fortified-wine casks. The ultimate after-dinner Irish?

Bushmills Malt 21-year-old 'Madeira Finish'

Already matured for nearly twenty years in a mix of American oak barrels and oloroso sherry butts, this single malt was then finished for two to three years in Madeira wood. The first bottling has been a huge success. It looks like this is an experiment that will be repeated.

Nose: It takes a while to open, but when warmed in the palm for a while there is a really warm glow of toasting almonds and baking raisins.

Taste: My tongue is firing off in all directions. There is stuff going on here I have never experienced before. Perfume, but heavier and oilier than I would expect and, at the back of it all, those slightly burnt bits you get on the edge of a Christmas cake.

Finish: Delicious. Winey.

Comments: This is a huge whiskey. Armed with a thesaurus, you would still have a hard time describing all the pleasures that lie in a glass. Without a doubt, the most fun you can have with your clothes on.

Bushmills Millennium Single Cask

Individual casks set down in 1982, then bottled at seventeen years old in American oak. This whiskey is sold at cask strength and has not been chill-filtered.

As with all bottlings from single barrels, the whiskey will vary somewhat from bottle to bottle. I tasted bottle number sixty-six from cask number 18401, at 51.6% abv.

Nose: Incredibly fruity. Mostly damsons, greengages and plums, but there are also Bartlett pears and freshly sliced pineapples. Wonderful.

Taste: Not at all what I was expecting. This is a dry, rather than a sweet, whiskey, which opens up like a flower, delivering silky malt and gentle cereal. Air produces spicy high notes that change even as you taste them.

Finish: After all that went before, the finish is a little shorter than I hoped it would be. Still a great buzzing climax to a thrilling ride.

Comments: This is a huge whiskey that shows just how good Bushmills malt can be when aged to perfection in decent American oak.

Bushmills 1608

Launched in October 1992, this was the first Irish whiskey to be designed exclusively for the booming duty-free trade. Then a twelve-year-old blend, it was re-formulated, re-packaged and re-released in the summer of 2001 without an age statement.

Nose: A pleasantly spicy, yet distinctly malty, nose.

Taste: Nice and fat on the tongue, which it tickles very gently, before turning to fudgy toffee with the sweetness of condensed milk.

Finish: Dark chocolate, slightly bitter, yet strangely sweet and dry.

Comments: Proof positive that age statements mean nothing. The new 1608 has the poise and balance that the twelve-year-old it replaces just didn't, and the finish is also off the top shelf. Brilliant stuff.

CLONTARF:

A charcoal-mellowed 'trinity' of Irish whiskeys.

Business partners Dave Phelan and Pat Rigney know a thing or two about the drinks industry. Former directors of R&A Bailey, they left the company shortly after their baby, Bailey's Whiskey, was smothered at birth. It is not a subject they like to talk about; in fact it is not something Bailey's like to talk about either. The wall of silence surrounding what should have been a dead–cert product, is deafening.

In September 1998 Dave and Pat's new company, Roaring Water Bay Spirits, launched the incredibly successful Ború vodka. 'Our mission statement is to market Irish spirit brands that are innovative, provocative, physically different and challenging,' says Dave Phelan. These words that would certainly apply to their next venture, Clontarf whiskey.

Pat remembers that the idea first struck him on a visit to the Jack Daniel's distillery in Tennessee. At Jack Daniel's, alcohol is 'charcoal mellowed', running from the still through twelve feet of maple charcoal.

If applying a technique from Tennessee to Irish Whiskey wasn't radical enough, the boys then went one better by marketing three different types of whiskey – single malt, special reserve (a blend) and regular black label (a grain whiskey) – in a single 'trinity' bottling. 'Why not?' says Dave. 'Like I keep telling people, we are in the entertainment business!' Each whiskey is also bottled separately.

Clontarf Single Malt

Nose: Tinned pears and custard.
Taste: The malt is very apparent – sweet, light and estery. The trademark Clontarf vanilla is next, and it quickly overpowers everything.
Finish: Short, with orangey ice cream.

Clontarf 'Special Reserve'

Nose: Spicy.
Taste: Quite fat and oily, with the malt and vanilla working well. However, it is the grain that holds this together, refusing to be drowned by the intense custard.
Finish: Bitter, with white chocolate. Very pleasant and complex.

Clontarf 'Black Label'

Nose: Citrus and heavy vanilla.
Taste: A wonderful marriage of firm grainy whiskey to smooth creamy-roundness.
Finish: Fudgy toffee and warming spice.
Comments: Like Tennessee whiskey, twice-distilled Irish grain whiskey can take charcoal mellowing. However, the unpeated Cooley malt used is already a mere wisp of a thing, and it just buckles under the onslaught of sweet vanilla. Of the three, the malt is the least impressive, but the other two are great session whiskeys.

COLERAINE DISTILLERY

'From Belfast we again started our "spiritual wanderings," and travelled by railway through towns and villages given up to the growth of flax and the manufacture of linens, until we came to the town of our quest, to pay a visit to the first "all malt" Distillery we have seen in Ireland.' Alfred Barnard, 1887

In Barnard's day, Coleraine and the Glen Distillery in North Cork were the only malt whiskey distilleries in the land. Even Bushmills, today renowned for its single malt, was producing the most popular drink in the Empire, pot still Irish whiskey.

Barnard singles out Coleraine, 'this famous malt distillery', for special mention. 'In all our wanderings through Erin's Green Isle, for cleanliness, order, and regularity, we have seen no distillery to beat this.' Although the distillery output was a tiny 100,000 gallons a year, its 'HC' brand still managed to hold up the shelves in the House of Commons in London.

By the 1920s, the distillery's fortunes had sadly waned. It lay idle until 1935, when William Boyd (son of Samuel Wilson Boyd, who, twelve years earlier, had acquired the Bushmills Distillery) bought the plant. When Isaac Wolfson took over the Boyd empire, he concentrated on the Bushmills brand, and Coleraine whiskey, in its own right, ceased to exist.

Coleraine

Nose: Woody spirit. Dull boot polish.

Taste: Honey softness. Tingly grain and bourbon oak.

Finish: Toffee and spice.

Comments: 'A lighter style of Bushmills whiskey,' is the corporate line, but in reality this is pretty rough stuff. The grain whiskey used in this blend is obviously very young, and there just isn't enough malt to keep it in check or give it any complexity.

Connemara

A peated single malt whiskey, Connemara used to be lightened with the addition of unpeated malt prior to bottling, but this is no longer the case. You now get 100 percent peated malt whiskey. Just as the Scots have colonised the world of malt whiskey and tried to make it their own, so too have they annexed the idea of peated malt. Their case has been helped by Irish Distillers who, in an attempt to put as much clear blue water between themselves and our Celtic cousins as possible, have occupied the land of triple-distillation. The truth, of course, is not as clear-cut. Prior to the arrival of Connemara, the last bastion of Irish peated malt whiskey was, in fact, Old Bushmills. As late as the 1960s, Austin Boyd, Chairman and Managing Director of the company, looked for 'sweetness, mellowness and overtones of peat' in his distillate.

Nose: A unique and hugely complex riot of sweet perfume and peat smoke. I'm standing near some honeysuckle on a still autumn night. Inside, the peat fire is being stoked.

Taste: Gently warming. Embers of turf toast the malt; the aroma then combines with silky rolls of oily, honeyed scents and rises into the nose.

Finish: Very smoky, like an old shebeen on the west coast, when the night is full and there's just a hint of a breeze through a far-off open window. This stuff would bring out the poet in anyone.

Comments: To equate Connemara with a peated Scottish malt is not to do it justice. Just as Ireland and Scotland are alike and yet different, those with an inclination towards Highland malts will find Connemara similar, yet different. There is no salt, iodine or heather here – this is a whiskey of the land.

Connemara Cask Strength

The cask strength version of Connemara is not chill-filtered, coloured or diluted in any way. Because of this, the level of alcohol differs between bottlings, and so labels are printed specially for each batch.

Nose: Cool fresh air blowing over a bed of mint. Ozone, camphor, turf.

Taste: Oily vanilla is first to take hold, followed by sweet, delicate cereal. All the while, the turf notes are rumbling along like far-off thunder.

Finish: Lightning strikes. Peppery chocolate and sparks of turf smoke spiral upwards. Then a cool zephyr of menthol. Magnificent.

Comments: This is one of the world's truly great whiskeys – drink it and weep.

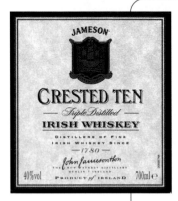

Crested Ten

A spicy, pot still blend, launched in 1963, this was the first Jameson product to be bottled solely by the distillery. Confusingly, the whiskeys featured in Crested Ten are not ten years old, but are largely matured for between seven and eight years. The whiskey is similar to Powers in having a fairly robust flavour, but here there is a strong sherry influence at work, which comes from first-fill oloroso casks.

Nose: There's linseed and fruit pudding, but very distant.

Taste: This is clearly Crested Ten, though the middle is a lot lighter than I remember. There's the signature hot, spicy pot still and this, combined with the rich dried fruit, makes this blend so unique.

Finish: Warming in an almost cough bottle way, though this falls off rapidly. A whiskey that is a lot calmer than I recall.

Comments: Not so long ago, the Crested Ten label got a much-needed makeover. It seems that the whiskey itself has also been altered, though not for the better.

An old bottling reveals a much heavier, oilier, spicy beast with a volcanic finish. It feels like the new Crested Ten has been made 'more approachable', i.e. blander. What a shame, as this really was a mother of a whiskey.

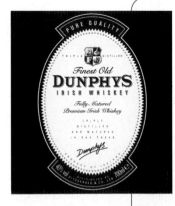

Dunphy's

This fairly young, grain-heavy blend was first launched in the 1950s by the Cork Distilleries Company, in partnership with a group of American importers who wanted to profit from the increasing interest in Irish coffee stateside. Shipped in bulk from Cork and bottled in America, at its peak Dunphy's sold 10,000 cases a year. It was withdrawn from sale in the USA in 1988, as part of Irish Distillers' decision to concentrate on marketing Jameson and Bushmills there. Today this whiskey is sold only in Ireland.

Nose: A hint of cereal.

Taste: A sweet start, which gives way to a watery middle and goes on to a bitter end. There's very little going on here.

Finish: Plastic aftertaste.

Comments: My concern is that the folks in marketing really think that Dunphy's et al are, 'a good introduction to the Irish whiskey range'. Just because these cheap brands taste of very little, doesn't mean they go down easily. Young, untamed grain whiskey can be pretty rough stuff. If I were given this on the nursery slopes of my Irish whiskey slalom, I think I would just give up.

Erin Go Bragh

This six-year-old is the only bottling of a Midleton single malt whiskey that I know of. The fact that Irish Distillers have not released it under their own banner, but rather sold it to an importer in Baltimore, Maryland, doesn't inspire confidence.

Nose: Brittle; nougat and spice.

Taste: Sweet and oily. It warms nicely, when cream pies laden with sherry come to the fore.

Finish: A peculiar and very dry vanilla tingle.

Comments: This is like no other malt I have ever tasted. In the blind tasting I was sure it was a pot still whiskey. Confused, I rang Barry Walsh, who said that the large Midleton Pot Stills seemed to be better for pot still rather than malt whiskey distillation. Erin go Bragh is a real curiosity, a malt that doesn't taste like a malt. This is a bottle for collectors, as I'm sure that from now on Midleton will keep their malt in-house, for blending purposes only.

Green Spot

A single pot still whiskey, bottled specifically for Mitchell & Son of Dublin, though also available from specialist whiskey outlets. Jonathan Mitchell is the fourth-generation guardian of this whiskey, one of Dublin's great treasures. His great-great-grandfather, Robert, started out as a whiskey bonder at the height of the Victorian whiskey boom, and Jonathan's son (also Robert) is standing in the wings, ready to take over.

In the days before accountants ruled the world, merchants like Mitchell & Son of Kildare Street would have vast stores of everything from whiskey to port maturing in their bonded stores. The most popular whiskey in the 'spot' range was always the ten-year-old Green Spot, but there were also Blue Spot (seven years old), Yellow Spot (twelve years old) and Red Spot (fifteen years old). This bewildering array of spots demanded an enormous amount of stock. So, when Irish Distillers stopped selling to the bonded trade, Mitchell's had enough whiskey laid down to keep Green Spot alive for ten years.

'Richard Burrows and I were both a lot younger back then,' says Jonathan Mitchell. 'I told him it would be foolish to let all the bonder brands die, because once they were gone, that was it!' Irish Distillers had a change of heart – no doubt they realised that some of the more famous bonded labels, like Redbreast and Green Spot, were valuable assets in themselves.

'Irish Distillers bought Green Spot from us,' says Jonathan. 'It was the only way we were going to keep the brand alive. They mature the stock in Midleton, but we have the sole rights to sell, market and develop the whiskey.' Green Spot is currently a vatting of seven- to twelve-year-old pot still whiskeys. No more than 2,000 six-bottle cases are produced each year.

Outside of Dublin's Kildare Street, finding a bottle of Green Spot isn't easy, but that's half the fun. When you do stumble across it, grab it with both hands and only let go to pour yourself a large measure.

Nose: The breathtaking crackle of pot still whiskey, infused with gentle wintergreen.

Taste: Full bodied with no apologies. Oily linseed cooled by strains of gentle menthol, joined by some spiciness towards the end.

Finish: Dry and sweet and long.

Comments: For those who like a slightly lighter pot still than that found in the older, more sherry-influenced Redbreast.

Greenore

Ireland's only distillery bottled single grain whiskey.

A mouthful of any Cooley blend (Millar's works best) shows the quality of their grain whiskey. Here, at eight years old, it is let out on its own.

Nose: Choc ice with a hint of cereal.

Taste: An almost salty start that gives way to buttery almonds. Light and sweet, but with a Jack Daniels-type clout and a fly-past of spice.

Finish: Fresh, with hints of vanilla and sugary coffee.

Comments: The most important thing to remember about Greenore is that it was never designed to have the complexity of a malt or pot still. This is a one-night stand – knock it back and get on with your short life.

Hennessy-na-Geanna

A single malt whiskey sold exclusively in Japan. *Na Géanna* is Irish for 'The Geese.'

In 1757 Richard Hennessy ended his military career and left his native Ireland with a certificate issued by his regiment attesting to his 'brave and gallant' nature.

Like many of his fellow 'Wild Geese', the native nobility who fled Ireland during the seventeenth and eighteenth centuries, Hennessy headed to Catholic France. In 1765 he established 'Hennessy, Conelly & Co' on the banks of the Charente River, in the heart of the Cognac region.

Today, this whiskey is the only non-cognac product to bear the Hennessy name. It was introduced 'to fight against the Japanese whiskeys which are taking the market share from Cognac,' according to Ives Tricoire, Hennessy Master Taster. 'We like the double-distillation, like we do with Cognac. We like the taste – not too simple. Also we like a lot of ageing.'

Nose: A gently smouldering turf fire; freshly baked, curranty soda bread.

Taste: A kiss of honeyed cereal and fragile vanilla and, behind it all, a spinning spiral of delicate, flowery peat smoke.

Finish: Glowing embers embrace the throat, spreading warmth out in all directions. This is an incredibly complex whiskey, beautifully constructed and matured to perfection. Simply a delicious, seductive ball of malt.

Comments: Softer and more refined than any other expression of Cooley's peated malt, Hennessy manages that most difficult trick of being, at the same time, both firm and gentle.

Hewitt's

A blend of Midleton and Bushmills malt whiskeys and Midleton grain whiskey.

In the consolidation that followed the foundation of the Cork Distilleries Company in 1868, the Watercourse Distillery, owned by the Hewitt family since 1793, fell silent. However, this distillery simply refused to die and, over the following century, it spluttered back to life on numerous occasions. The Hewitt name, it would seem, is as tenacious as the old distillery. Hewitt's whiskey made a comeback in the early 1960s when CDC tried something very bold. 'Hewitt's whisky, which has recently been placed on the Irish market is different,' reads a CDC internal memo from 1965. 'It is a malt and grain blend, and is therefore somewhat similar to many of the imported whiskies on sale in Ireland.' In other words, Hewitt's whisky (without the 'e') was a peated blend.

However, the experiment didn't work. After the formation of Irish Distillers, the whiskey was reformulated and gained an obligatory 'e'. Stubborn as ever, today this whiskey hangs on in pockets of regional loyalty – notably Limerick, Galway, Mayo and Donegal. Outside of these areas it is impossible to get.

Nose: Powerful oily nose. This is exactly what a whiskey warehouse smells like.

Taste: Bags of flavour assail the taste buds. Greengages give way to sultanas as the dried fruit turns into warming sherry spice.

Finish: Pleasant chocolate grain; very, very dry.

Comments: Hard to get hold of even in Ireland, this is a real box of delights and a genuine find. Well worth exploring on a cold winter's evening.

Inishowen

Ireland's only openly peated blend. Inishowen is Cooley's twist on a well-worn tale, first spun by Hewitt's over forty years ago. The logic is still sound – people like blended Scotch, so let's give them what they want. However, it seems that Ireland's whiskey drinkers are having a hard time getting used to a locally produced peated blend. Inishowen is thirty percent malt, with a distinctive peat character. The whiskey is matured half-and-half in bourbon first- and second-fill casks.

Nose: A warm plume of peat smoke and, behind that, some very soft and sweet cereal.

Taste: Very soft and mouth filling. As the whiskey warms, the peat recedes and the signature Cooley fruit comes to the fore.

Finish: Dry and yet complex, as the various elements wax and wane on the back of the tongue. When the peat finally dies, some very decent vanilla stays on the palate for ages.

Comments: A delightful whiskey, which deserves a wider audience.

JOHN JAMESON & SON

'The Bow Street Distillery, which is one of the oldest in Ireland, having been established in the year 1780, covers upwards of five acres of ground, and is a quarter of a mile from the Four Courts, and about half a mile from Sackville Street, credited with being the broadest street in Europe.'

Alfred Barnard, 1887

Like most things to do with Irish whiskey, the further back in time you go the mistier the details become. What we do know about John Jameson is that he was a Scottish Presbyterian who came to Ireland and took over an existing distillery in around 1780.

For the next 200 years, until 1988 in fact, there was always a descendant of John Jameson working for the company in the same offices at Bow Street in Dublin. Each generation of Jamesons built on the success of the last, until JJ&S was recognised as the finest whiskey money could buy. It would seem that very dull history makes for very good whiskey.

Ripples first began to appear in the calm waters of Bow Street towards the end of the nineteenth century, with the rise of blended whiskey. By 1891 the unthinkable had happened – profits had started to slip.

By 1902 John Jameson & Son had become a public company. Three years later, just as the London Borough of Islington started the legal steps that would legitimise the Coffey still, John Jameson IV retired. His replacement was Andrew Jameson, without whose leadership it is doubtful the company would have survived the turbulence that was about to swamp the Irish industry.

Andrew Jameson was a colourful character. He briefly ran a brewery and then, at the depressingly young age of thirty-two, was made a director of the Bank of Ireland. Andrew was a staunch Unionist, who also served in the Free State Senate, and for thirty-six years he steered the company through some of its darkest days. Not without a sense of humour, prior to his death in 1941 Andrew reflected: 'I'm lucky to be alive. All my friends died young, of drink. They were drinking brandy and soda, you see.'

The company survived the lean 1940s and 1950s, and entered the swinging 'sixties in a bullish mood. Jameson cut its links with the bonded whiskey trade and started bottling its own product, a move that Chairman Aleck Crichton rightly described as 'the most important decision that has been taken since the distillery was founded in 1780.' The Bow Street distillery finally closed in 1971. When Irish Distillers was taken over by Groupe Pernod Ricard in 1988, Jameson was singled out for greatness.

In 1996 Jameson was the world's fastest growing spirit brand: sales finally broke through the magic one-million-cases-a-year barrier and the whiskey joined the world's top 100 spirit brands. Today Jameson is synonymous with Irish whiskey, and is sold in over 100 countries. The old Bow Street distillery, where the whole story began, has been restored and now houses a heritage centre. In an industry that has suffered so much destruction and sadness, it is nice to have at least one happy ending.

Jameson

The world's largest-selling Irish whiskey.

In the 1970s, when the American market was reported as finding the Jameson of the period a bit too oily and heavy, the company gave in to the inevitable. More than 100 years after the birth of blended Scotch, Ireland's greatest whiskey house followed suit. Jameson shifted from being a pure pot still whiskey to a blend, a process known as 'managed change'. Currently Jameson is a blend of roughly fifty percent medium-bodied pot still and fifty percent grain whiskey. It is matured in first-fill bourbon and sherry wood, for between four and seven years.

Nose: Refreshing, spicy nose with gentle toasted woodiness. Very enticing.

Taste: Good, firm body. Warming oiliness, with some distant citrus notes. Light sherry follows up the rear, keeping the grain on a firm lead.

Finish: Long and dry, with a peppery kick and a buzz of sherry. A very, very pleasant way to spend a quiet moment.

Comments: I was surprised when this whiskey was revealed to be Jameson. Like cornflakes, I thought Jameson was something I'd passed through on the way to muesli and limited editions. However, this is a whiskey of great charm and finesse. As iconic as the Rock of Cashel or the Ha'penny Bridge, Jameson is a classic and a great way into the world of Irish.

Jameson 1780

The use of fresh bourbon barrels in addition to the judicious use of sherry wood gives the pot still whiskeys in 1780 real character. More sherried and older than Crested Ten, featuring whiskeys that are at least twelve years old, it is typically around eighty percent pot still whiskey, twenty percent grain whiskey.

Nose: A not-unpleasant combination of motor oil and leather. Is this what a warm evening in Jerez smells like?

Taste: Very sweet and gentle. This is beautifully balanced; nothing is overstated. If whiskey is classical music, here we are dealing with Wolfgang Amadeus Mozart. There are lots of cream pies and rich oloroso notes, but also some very old pot still, which eventually dominates. When the grain does arrive it has, as you would expect, slowed to a blur.

Finish: The sherry melts into lip-smacking milk chocolate.

Comments: Jameson 1780 is simply a beautiful whiskey, and has to rate in the world's top five blends. It is also excellent value for money, more than able to hold its own against whiskeys costing ten times as much. It will therefore not come as a huge shock to learn that this whiskey is the preferred choice of Barry Walsh and Barry Crockett.

Jameson 12-year-old 'Distillery Reserves'

These are aged Jameson variants, available only at the Midleton and Old Jameson distillery heritage centres.

Midleton Distillery Reserve

A close cousin of Jameson 1780, but with a more pronounced sherry-cask flavour.
Nose: Stewed dried fruits.
Taste: A vibrant dance of juicy pot still, sultanas and dark brown sugar.
Finish: Hot and fruity – cinnamon, cloves and allspice. Wonderfully evocative.
Comments: A winning digestive, especially in winter. A personal favourite.

Old Jameson Distillery Reserve

Also related to Jameson 1780, but just a little bit older on average and more full-flavoured.
Nose: Subtle vanilla and caramel sweetness.
Taste: A salty start, then boiled sweets and honey throat lozenges.
Finish: Pepper and spice. Custard Cream biscuits and mulled wine.
Comments: Distillery Reserves are known in the industry as 'trophy bottles'. Tourists usually buy them as a holiday souvenir, in rather the same way your auntie brought home that dodgy bottle of prune brandy from Spain. So full marks to Irish Distillers for not taking the easy option and actually putting something decent into the drinks cabinets of our foreign cousins.

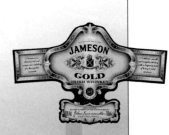

Jameson Gold

A deluxe blend of selected casks of Jameson whiskey, up to twenty years old and featuring, uniquely, some whiskey matured in new virgin oak barrels. This imparts a particular flavour which Barry Walsh describes as 'honey toasted sweetness'. Originally designed for Far East duty-free shops, it is now readily available in Ireland.
Nose: A delicate waft of honeysuckle and biscuits.
Taste: Very viscous. Oily sweetness is the key here, with sticky-sweet fruit and sweet cream riding over the more delicate malt and cereal. Some piquant notes do manage to get through.
Finish: Firm and quite long, especially the winey notes, which seem to cling to every crevice of the mouth.
Comments: This is the Citizen Kane of the Irish whiskey world. Critics rave until they foam at the mouth, but I just don't get it. For me, this has more in common with a liqueur than a whiskey. Even as I write this, I can feel the enamel on my teeth being eaten away. But whiskeys are as individual as we are, and if Citizen Kane does it for you, then it is quite possible that you will find lots to enjoy here.

Jameson Pure Pot Still

Limited edition pot still whiskey. This expression of Jameson 15-year-old is considerably less oily than its historical predecessor of some thirty or so years ago. The current bottling, distilled in the mid-1980s, shows how Irish Distillers have narrowed the cut retained from the final distillation, thus producing a lighter pot still spirit.

Nose: There are those (and you know who you are) who scoff at descriptives like 'damp raincoats'. Well, you will be relieved to know that here the nose is lighter; still mushroom-musty and sweet, yet cut with that wonderful pot still thyme and spearmint.

Taste: Harder than the nose would lead you to believe. Tongue-tingling oily linseed and walnuts, warmed by a hint of winey extract, though there isn't the usual sherry sweetness – it's more like dark mint chocolate.

Finish: Bitter and dry.

Comments: This bottling contains some of the heaviest pot still whiskeys produced in Midleton. The considerable use of sherry wood is obvious, though not at all overpowering. The Jameson 15 year-old is drier than Redbreast – more like an ancient and more full-bodied Green Spot.

Kilbeggan

Cooley distillery's best-selling brand.

This whiskey takes its name from the midlands town, once home to Locke's Distillery, where Cooley now mature their whiskey.

Noel Sweeney and ex-Chivas blender Jimmy Lang had quite a job on their hands to put together this blend. As they set to work in 1994, the Cooley Distillery had been mothballed, the workers had been let go and there were very limited supplies of whiskey to draw on. There was some young malt but, critically, the grain whiskey was barely legal, as the continuous stills had only started operating in September 1990. As the stocks of whiskey at Noel Sweeney's disposal have expanded and matured, so Kilbeggan has shifted in shape and style. The latest incarnation was launched in the winter of 2001. Now Kilbeggan is a blend of around thirty percent five- to six-year-old malt whiskey, seventy percent seven- to ten-year-old grain. The whiskeys are matured in a mixture of fresh and first-fill bourbon wood.

Nose: A real winner. Boiled sweets and juicy tinned pineapple.

Taste: Very round and complex. This whiskey instantly fills every corner of the mouth with honey on toast. Oaky grains follow, but they are very well behaved schoolboys.

Finish: Chocolate-covered coffee beans.

Comments: Noel Sweeney tells me that Kilbeggan was 'tweaked' for its recent brand makeover. I would use stronger words, like 'changed beyond recognition'. This is a really grown-up whiskey, beautifully constructed and wonderfully executed. If Cooley get their marketing together, this is one to take on Jameson.

KNAPPOGUE CASTLE:

Vintage bottlings of Irish whiskey.

The current President of American company Great Spirits, owners of the Knappogue Castle brand, is Mark Andrews, whose father set the ball rolling in the 1930s.

Though not of Irish descent, Mark Edwin Andrews loved the country and during the 1920s and 1930s he made numerous visits here. By the early 1960s, his fortune made, he bought the ruined Knappogue Castle, near Shannon airport in County Clare.

Andrews also had a passion for Irish whiskey, and purchased as many casks of the Tullamore 1951 vintage as the distillery would sell him. These he stored in a Cork warehouse. In 1987, after being in sherry wood for thirty-six years, the whiskey was finally bottled. Generous to a fault, Mark Edwin Andrews gave it away as presents to his friends and family.

Ten years later, his son brought the remaining bottles to the USA and put them up for sale. The response was such that Mark decided to repeat the experiment and launched the Knappogue Castle brand.

To date, four modern vintages exist – 1990 to 1993 inclusive – with the first three years coming from the Cooley Distillery; the 1993 hails from Old Bushmills. The 1990 and 1991 vintages are no longer available.

Knappogue Castle 1951

A pure pot still whiskey, bottled in 1987 at thirty-six years old.

Nose: Oilskins and leather, clover and heavy black fruit. The wonderful and unmissable kick of old pot still whiskey.

Taste: Oily sweetness opens to reveal oaky vanilla, then the honey returns with an almost lemony tingle on the tip of the tongue. Hints of sherry and finally firm, though never overpowering, wood.

Finish: The pot still is amazingly fresh and fruity, then the oak tannin takes a final bow. Bravo!

Comments: This is one of the truly great Irish whiskeys. The Tullamore distillery has made way for a shopping mall, but the pot stills that gave this spirit life now sit in Kilbeggan and are the property of Cooley Distillery's Dr John Teeling. If he ever follows through on his plan to fire them up, this will surely be the greatest resurrection since Lazarus.

Knappogue Castle 1992

A single malt whiskey, bottled in 2000 at eight years old.

Nose: Zesty lemons, bouquets of flowers and the trademark Cooley fruit bowl. Intense and winning, we're off to a good start here.

Taste: Waves of honeycomb malt, tempered by some very decent but gentle wood. Tyrconnell with the volume turned up to eleven.

Finish: Biscuits and clover, with vanilla moving towards the end to give a buttery kiss.

Comments: This vintage illustrates just how good Cooley's unpeated malt can be when given a bit longer in the wood.

Knappogue Castle 1993

A single malt, bottled in 2001 at eight years old.

Nose: Buttery almonds and delicate malt. When it warms there are some welcome estery notes and delicate vanilla.

Taste: Very light. It doesn't take a lot of water to kill this baby stone dead. Fresh glass in hand, and it takes a while before the distillate springs to life – maybe springs is too strong a word, it's more like a waft really. I'm afraid 'winey cereal' is the best I can come up with.

Finish: Watery oatmeal.

Comments: The already light, triple-distilled malt has been matured in decent but unexciting bourbon barrels, so we're left with a vintage that doesn't have a lot to say for itself. It would seem perhaps that Bushmills hang on to their best stuff?

LOCKE'S BRUSNA DISTILLERY

'To the music of the fiddle and a banjo, two Irish lads, regular "broths of boys," were dancing and shouting, and at times their movements were so infectious that some of the crowd joined in with them. An Irishman is always ready to fall into a jig, and the sound of music will generally set him off … But we had business before us, and soon parted from the revellers, having first parted with some silver, being unable to refuse the blarney appeals of these rustic musicians.' Alfred Barnard, 1887

Visit the Brusna Distillery at Kilbeggan today and you will be stepping back in time. This is not a museum – it is a time warp, for the distillery is, more or less, just as Barnard saw it all those years ago. The reason is simple – Locke's was a small, pot still operation; they never installed a Coffey still and there was never enough money to update the buildings, most of which date from the eighteenth century.

In 1843, when John Locke initially leased the Brusna Distillery, it was already a going concern, having been established in 1757 by Matthew McManus. When John Locke and his family arrived in Kilbeggan the industry was already in recession, and Locke had just recently extracted himself from a failed whiskey venture in Tullamore.

Under John Edward and James Harvey Locke, grandsons of its founder, the Kilbeggan distillery enjoyed a period of expansion. New buildings were erected, and turnover grew as whiskey was transported all over the country by canal and rail. Locke's pot still was famous for its good body and intense flavour, and was a favourite of blenders. In 1908 almost 18,000 gallons of mature whiskey went north to the blending houses of Belfast – here it would be mixed with locally produced 'silent spirit' before being sold on under a variety of labels.

However, the small family concern was not immune to the plague of closures that decimated the industry in the 1920s. Like its neighbour in Tullamore, it rode out the worst by simply pulling down the shutters. In 1924 the already old-fashioned distillery was mothballed for seven long years, and when it reopened there was no money to update anything.

The two remaining members of the Locke family – sisters Flo and Sweet, who at the time ran the distillery – had no interest in the business. With post-war whiskey stocks rising in value, they put the distillery up for sale. An international consortium attempted to buy the company, but when a promised £75,000 deposit never materialised, questions started to be asked. A local politician accused members of the government of being part of a shady plan to sell the distillery to foreigners. Accusations of bribery went as high as the taoiseach, Eamon de Valera. Although nothing was ever proven, the Locke's scandal was one of the factors that led to the downfall of the government a year later.

Crippled with debt and diminishing sales, in 1953 Kilbeggan distilled for the last time. Five years later, the company went into receivership and, in 1963, the remaining whiskey stocks and the distillery were sold to a German pig farmer, Karl Heinz Mellor.

Mellor made a lot of money in Germany, selling aged Locke's pot still under the name Old Galleon. He also smashed thousands of Locke's whiskey crocks and used them as a base for new concrete floors, turning centuries-old warehouses into pigsties. Luckily though, much of the plant was left intact.

In 1982 the local community leased the distillery from Powerscreen, its new owners, who had run a Volvo dealership from the premises. A major renovation project was undertaken; the buildings were weatherproofed and the waterwheel was made functional. Cooley bought most of the site in 1987 and, although distilling no longer takes place in Kilbeggan, the old buildings are once again alive with the smell of maturing whiskey and the sound of coopers at work.

But the story may not end there: 'Out the back there are three pot stills.' Cooley founder John Teeling's eyes flash with the kind of challenge this man seems to need to get through the day. He is referring to the mighty pot stills from Tullamore that sit where the scrapped Locke's stills used to. 'One day I'd just love to get them working. To produce a handcrafted whiskey on a small scale ...' He drifts off. With John Teeling anything is possible.

Locke's Blend

A blend with a higher malt content than its stablemate, Kilbeggan.
Locke's blend has a thirty-five percent malt whiskey content, with a hint of that being peated. 'Peat enhances the flavour of whiskey in rather the same way that salt brings out the taste of food,' says Master Blender Noel Sweeney. 'You won't taste the peat in the finished blend, as it is used like a condiment.' The grain is matured in first- and second-fill bourbon casks.
Nose: Ripe pears and a hint of turf.
Taste: Sharp citrus with a sweet follow-through. Toasted wood.
Finish: A lovely mint-Aero moment.
Comments: This was once the more charming of the two brands, but Kilbeggan has now left this whiskey standing.

Locke's 8-year-old Blend

Produced exclusively for the German market.
Nose: Peat covering citrus.
Taste: Malty to begin with, then comes an uncoordinated rabble of grainy, metallic distillate.
Finish: Rough and unpleasant.
Comments: This limited bottling is unlikely to be repeated, which is just as well.

Locke's Single Malt, 8-year-old

Limited bottlings of this lightly peated malt are made on a regular basis.
Locke's malt uses some of the oldest available malt whiskey in the warehouses, giving the brand a characteristic woody flavour. Single malts can return a margin of up to four times that of blended whiskey, so brands like this are a crucial part of the company's future profitability.
Nose: Powerful pear drops and candied pineapple, carried on a gentle breeze of turf smoke.
Taste: Very complex and subtle. It is so well constructed that separating the various elements is not easy. There's the usual Cooley spicy sweetness, but this time overlaid by custard and peat. Wonderful.
Finish: Long, with peat again, then a wonderful biscuity dryness. Then more lingering warm peat.
Comments: This whiskey was recently reformulated and the results are stunning. The original Locke's malt was a confusion of instruments playing different tunes. This time, however, the orchestra has well and truly got its act together. Music to the taste buds.

MIDLETON DISTILLERY

'We drove up the centre of the big quadrangle, and through a crowd of carts and waggons laden with corn. The farmers were busy offering their samples, while among the crowd were several groups of laughing girls, who had accompanied their friends for the sake of an outing.' Alfred Barnard, 1887

The big quadrangle still exists in front of the Old Midleton Distillery, though these days these the carts have been replaced by coaches and the laughing girls are as likely to be from Paris, Milan or New York as from Cork.

Today there are two distilleries in Midleton. The beautiful old Victorian building described by Barnard is now a heritage centre bustling with tourists. Behind it lies the utilitarian new Midleton distillery, where most Irish Distillers brands are created.

Distilling on this site goes back to 1825, when the Murphy brothers – James, David and Jeremiah – bought the site for the princely sum of £4,000. They soon established a thriving distillery, and family members branched into brewing with equal success. Murphy's stout is still produced in Cork City.

In 1867 Midleton Distillery amalgamated with four other local operations, to form the Cork Distilleries Company (CDC). Over time, CDC centralised all production at the Midleton plant. It was a taste of things to come. In 1966 CDC was one of the founding members of Irish Distillers and, yet again, all production was moved to Cork. In 1975 the old Midleton Distillery, like its former rivals in Bow Street and John's Lane, was closed, and a brand new, state-of-the-art distillery was opened. The new Midleton plant was nothing less than the ark the Irish hoped would carry them to better times. It was a last-ditch attempt at survival.

The new Midleton distillery was designed to have the capacity to replicate the output of the plants it replaced. It would have to produce the new-style Jameson, Powers and Paddy whiskeys, as well as vodka and gin. Luckily for us, the gamble paid off.

Dungourney 1964 Pure Pot Still

A pure pot still whiskey from the original Midleton Distillery, bottled in 1994 at thirty years old. For thirty long years, a cask of pot still whiskey lay undisturbed in a corner of Midleton warehouse number eleven. While it slumbered, CDC ceased to exist, Irish Distillers was formed, the stills that gave birth to the whiskey went cold and in their shadow a new distillery was opened, which was subsequently bought by the French. In all that time, no one even knew that this whiskey existed.

When found, the remarkable survivor was bottled and christened Dungourney after the river that, three decades earlier, had given part of itself up to the spirit.

Nose: Leather and ferns in the rain, though still very light and attractive.

Taste: Oily on the tongue and robust in flavour. This pot still whiskey is both viscous and sweet, but balancing that are some cool notes and a hint of *crème brûlée*.

Finish: A gentle giant. Both honey-sweet and biscuity, with the unmalted barley making itself felt towards the end. Long and very pleasant.

Comments: Remarkably fresh and youthful for an Irish that has spent so long in the wood. This was clearly an exceptional cask, though not on its first or second outing as there is hardly any wood astringency – just light vanilla. Outstanding.

Midleton 25-year-old Pure Pot Still

A one-off bottling of pot still whiskey from the old Midleton distillery, distilled in September 1973 and aged for twenty-five years in oloroso butts.

Nose: Very dense and complex. Brittle linseed, sharp sherry and burnt toffee.

Taste: Incredibly fat and oily; rich sweetness is followed by spices tossed on a hot skillet. Only towards the end is age evident, but the slight mustiness works brilliantly when played off against the stark pot still.

Finish: Initially very soft and gentle; only when it has gone down do some toasted custard and sherry come through.

Comments: This is an experience every Irish whiskey aficionado should undertake at least once in a lifetime. Now I understand why one retired distillery worker said, 'You could live on that old Midleton whisky.' Those huge pot stills produced some epic distillate, helped, no doubt, by the inclusion of oats in the grist.

Midleton 26-year-old Pure Pot Still

A one-off bottling, released to celebrate the 175th anniversary of the old Midleton distillery. Some of the twenty-five-year-old pot still whiskey was finished for an extra year in a single port pipe.

Nose: Winey pot still and, behind that, oaky vanilla.

Taste: Wrapped in a blanket of overripe plums comes a package of pungent pot still. However, the fresh port doesn't sit too well with the ancient oak.

Finish: The fortified wine is clearly evident at the start, before giving way to the brooding wood.

Comments: A strange animal, though for my money the various elements don't quite hang together.

Midleton 30-year-old Pure Pot Still

Just two original barrels of this whiskey survived in the old stone warehouses in Midleton, and after thirty years in the wood they realised just 300 bottles. Almost half of the spirit laid down in 1969 had evaporated.

Nose: A dark baritone note of humming tangerines, molasses and freshly sliced ginger. Round and pendulous.

Taste: Spicy with damp mushrooms, though it is the almost bitter cereal that really makes itself felt. Later, sweet, earthy elements come into play. The distillate and the maturation are clearly locked in a battle to the death.

Finish: The cask wins hands down. The pot still gives up and is beaten to death with staves of splintery timber.

Comments: As an object lesson in the evils of over-maturation, it is interesting to compare this whiskey with Dungourney, both from the same distillery and bottled at thirty years old. After an age in wood, there can be very little difference between ancient whiskey, rum and brandy. They all share the same wood-derived characteristics, which eventually overpower the distillate. I'm afraid that is what has happened here, although it hasn't in the case of Dungourney. A classic example of how 'old' doesn't always equal 'better'.

Midleton VR 2001

Midleton Very Rare is one of the most expensive whiskeys produced on a regular basis by Irish Distillers. Rarely more, and usually rather less, than 2,500 cases of Midleton VR have been released annually since 1984. Older vintages feature whiskey from the silent old Midleton distillery; more recent bottlings are the work of the new distillery. Barry Walsh says that his objective each year is 'to produce the best whiskey possible'. The 2001 vintage contains a range of whiskeys aged between twelve and twenty-five years. It is slightly milder than Redbreast, as it is a blend. This is a whiskey that Barry likes to drink neat, with just a dash of water to open the nose.

Nose: The alluring smell of a freshly beeswaxed drinks cabinet.

Taste: Full and honeyed malt, melon and the fluffy bit in the middle of a walnut whip.

Finish: There's no trace of any grain, just layers of cream soda and soft whiskey. Only at the very end is there any hint of wood, and then it is a gentle tickle of aged vanilla. This goes down very easily – simply a sublime Irish.

Comments: If master blenders bring their personalities to bear on their work, then Midleton VR is Barry Walsh in a glass. This is a softly-spoken gentleman of a whiskey. Discreet and complex, you could easily while the night away in its company. Expensive in Ireland, good value in duty free, buy Midleton VR overseas or in a pub and you will think you're paying into the Irish Distillers' pension fund.

Millar's Special Reserve

A weighty, sherried blend.

Adam Millar & Company was a firm of Dublin whiskey bonders, which sat across the road from Power's. Cooley Distillery bought them out in 1988.

Millar's has a twenty percent malt content, with both grain and malt having been aged in first-fill bourbon casks. This gives the brand extra weight, as do some sherry notes. This was Noel Sweeney's first solo blend, and remains his favourite.

Nose: Firm malt with a sherry accent.

Taste: A fat, oily whiskey, and much heavier than the usual Cooley offerings. The grain is clearly evident, but this is a well-constructed blend and everything hangs together beautifully.

Finish: Unlike many grain-heavy blends, there is no nasty afterburn. Instead, you get a fabulous, tingly cough-bottle kind of finish. Loads of liquorice and vanilla, which hang around for ages.

Comments: Until the Kilbeggan makeover, this was my favourite Cooley blend by far. While there is a lot of grain in the brand, for once the completed whiskey doesn't try to be light and inoffensive. Try having just the one – Millar's is dangerously moreish.

Murphy's

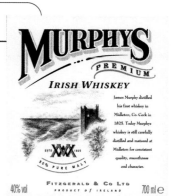

Somewhat similar to Dunphy's, but with a little more malty character.

Designed as a cheaper bulk blend to allow CDC to compete in the Irish Coffee market, at its peak Murphy's Irish whiskey sold more than 80,000 cases a year. Like Dunphy's, it was withdrawn from sale in the USA in 1988. Today it is sold solely in Ireland.

Nose: Distant malt with hints of buttery bourbon oak.

Taste: More butter and a lot of vanilla melt into some toffee. This isn't hugely complex, but it is enjoyable.

Finish: The grain can clearly be felt on the back of the tongue, leaving some praline behind and a slightly spirity aftertaste.

Comments: Simple, and quite fun for those who like a light, refreshing whiskey.

Old Dublin

Largely a grain whiskey, but charmed with a touch of pot still. Matured in refill casks on their third or even fourth outing, the whiskeys are young, at just over three years old.

This is one of several value-for-money brands marketed by Irish Distillers. In truth, whiskeys like Old Dublin don't really offer the consumer value for money. Duty on seven-year-old pot still whiskey, matured in first-fill bourbon casks, is the same as the duty on three-year-old grain whiskey matured in an old boot.

Nose: Vague vanilla.

Taste: Lots of assertive grain. Not at all unpleasant – just a little one-dimensional, as a single note is all that ever arrives.

Finish: Firm, grainy cocoa.

Comments: When, for not much more than the price of a bottle of Old Dublin, you could enjoy a world-class brand like Jameson, why buy this?

Paddy

During the 1920s and 1930s, there were two whiskeys which could easily be bought by the bottle in Ireland. The first was Powers Gold Label. The second was Cork Distilleries Company Old Irish Whisky, which, as good as it might have been when it slipped down the throat, was not the easiest brand name to trip off the tongue.

My mother remembers talk of the larger-than-life Paddy Flaherty, CDC sales representative, riding into Mitchelstown and buying drinks for anyone old enough to hold a glass (although she assures me she is far too young to have ever met the man). Before long people were asking for his whiskey by name: 'Paddy Flaherty's whisky'.

In those days of counterfeit brands, it wasn't long before CDC put Paddy's signature at the foot of the label to show that theirs was the real thing. Then, by degree, the label altered until the whiskey was eventually called, quite simply, Paddy.

In those days, Paddy was a very different animal to what it is today. 'There was eating and drinking in it,' remembers Sean O'Mahony of Cork's North Mall bottling plant. 'You'd need a knife and fork to get through the stuff!'

Today's Paddy features slightly older whiskeys than are found in Jameson, and although there is a similar wood policy, Paddy does not use as much first-fill wood. This whiskey also features a small amount of Bushmills malt, which really comes into play on the excellent nose. Otherwise, the whiskey is made up of roughly equal measures of pot still whiskey and grain whiskey.

Nose: Lovely. Delicate flowers.

Taste: Surprisingly sweet and perfumy, this whiskey opens up nicely if sloshed around the mouth.

Finish: Dry, the grain behaving itself to leave a pleasant aftertaste.

Comments: Everything about this whiskey is light and airy. Very elegant indeed, though it works best with just a drop of water.

JOHN POWER & SON

'Our next day's expedition was to John's Lane Distillery, which is situated a short distance from Christchurch Cathedral. Soon after starting we had our first experience of an Irish shower, and received on our devoted heads some portion of the heavy libations poured on "Ould Ireland," which make her fields so marvellously green; they made us look ruefully blue. Fortunately it did not last long, and by the time we reached our destination the sun shone brightly.' Alfred Barnard, 1887

The Power's distillery sat just south of the River Liffey, rubbing elbows with the Guinness brewery and facing its great rival, John Jameson and Son, across a narrow and often smelly band of green water.

James Power opened a small distillery in around 1791. By century's end his son John had joined him, and they took up residence in John's Lane. John Power took over the company in 1817 and became a very influential man in the capital – for a number of years he was high sheriff of Dublin and he was a close friend of Daniel O'Connell, the Liberator. At the age of sixty-four he became Sir John Power, and could look back on a successful life, having extended his distillery until it covered seven acres of the inner city.

Always the innovators, the distillery-bottled Gold Label brand was a huge success. Soon, though, Dublin wags had re-christened it 'three swallows' – not after the trio of birds that appear on the label, but after the way in which the spirit is best taken: 'in three swallows'.

Like every other distillery on the island, Power's felt the combined blows of the Economic War, Depression, American Prohibition and political mismanagement.

In the 1950s, ostensibly for the production of neutral grain spirit to supply their newly launched Powers Gin and Saratov Vodka brands, the company installed a continuous still. However, recognising the inevitable world trend away from heavy pot still whiskey, production director Clem Ryan (the Power line crossed to the female side of the family when Gwendaline Anna Power married Major General Ryan) was soon experimenting with distilling lighter whiskey types. These made their way imperceptibly into Gold Label in the 1960s, and it ceased to be branded 'pure pot still'.

Powers Gold Label

The biggest-selling whiskey in Ireland.

Ireland's most popular whiskey is a spicy, oily animal, with a hard underbelly that comes from seventy to eighty percent pot still whiskey. Interestingly, though, this is medium pot still whiskey, not heavy as you might expect. Older than Jameson, this whiskey uses a fair proportion of refill casks, as Powers is 'distillate driven', with less cask-derived flavour than in other brands.

Nose: A belter of a nose. It is easy to spot the signature pot still cereal coming from the unmalted barley. There's honey and spice and all things nice. Ravishing.

Taste: A carnival of taste sensations grips the tongue. This is clearly Powers, so whatever you do, don't sip. The only way to drink it is in big loud gulps. Suck in some air – honey, heather and allspice are released. Then swallow.

Finish: Long and lingering. Start over.

Comments: Powers Gold Label is simply a brilliant whiskey. If you are broke and can buy just one bottle of Irish, make it Powers Gold Label.

Powers 12-year-old 'Special Reserve'

A limited edition aged expression.

The whiskey formulation for Powers Gold Label, and that for the 12-year-old Special Reserve, is exactly the same. The whiskeys here are simply older – twelve years rather than the four to seven years of the standard blend.

Nose: Hard spice, crushed nuts and a hint of dried porcini.

Taste: Lots of pot still, sherry wood and gentle sweetness. Next up comes a freshly opened jar of honey and, finally, fiery cereal and cooling custard. This is a complex whiskey, though the age, so obvious on the nose, is not apparent in the taste.

Finish: A tingling chilli-like sensation, followed by linseed and ginger.

Comment: If you like heavier Irish whiskeys like Powers Gold Label, then you would be a fool to miss this baby. Extra time in the cask means this expression has even more of what you drink Powers for, namely body and flavour. At the same time, the wood has softened some of Gold Label's harder edges. Initially produced in limited quantities for the Millennium, this is excellently priced and some vintages are now scarce.

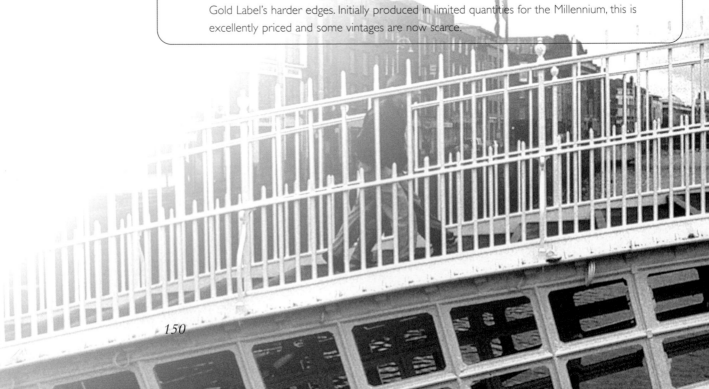

Redbreast Pure Pot Still 12-year-old

A continuation of the great tradition of pure Irish pot still whiskeys, made from a mixture of malted and unmalted barley. Harder and oilier than other whiskeys, Redbreast is aged for at least twelve years, mostly in sherry wood, though some fresh bourbon wood is also used. Redbreast was the name bonders Gilbey's of Ireland gave to Jameson distillate that they matured and bottled in the early part of the twentieth century. When the bonder trade was phased out in 1968, Gilbey's made a special plea to be allowed to continue to supply Redbreast, and small quantities were in circulation throughout the 1970s and 1980s. In the 1990s, Irish Distillers bought the brand from Gilbey's and relaunched Redbreast as a twelve-year-old.

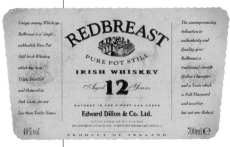

Nose: Some blends may have 'pot still character', but this is where you can experience the real thing. A pot still nose offers a very inviting combination of resin and linseed, sherry and cream soda. A unique experience.

Taste: Fat and oily, the use of unmalted barley in this pot still whiskey gives Redbreast a hard edge that snaps the taste buds into life. Thereafter the flavours keep unfolding – from easy ones like ginger and fruitcake to others I can't even find words for. There is nothing for it, you will just have to buy a bottle to see what I mean.

Finish: Long and lingering, with some classy sherry rounding off a magnificent performance. Is this the best whiskey in the world?

Comments: Imagine a time when whiskeys like Redbreast were not the exception, but the norm. It makes me want to cry.

Redbreast Pot Still Blend

Nose: Almost nothing.

Taste: A weak, watery start, then the back of the tongue is tickled by some sherry notes. However, they quickly die away, to be replaced by spirity grain.

Finish: A hint of cough bottle.

Comments: Just how this mess is meant to be 'an introduction to the more full-flavoured single pot still expression,' is beyond me. This whiskey has as much in common with its namesake as whiskey writer Michael Jackson has with his. Whoever had the bright idea of extending the Redbreast family should be locked in a padded cell before they can do any more damage. I mean, can you imagine Ferrari putting their name on a Trabant? Even blind, this whiskey is pretty awful, but as it bears the Redbreast name, it is an utter disgrace.

TULLAMORE DISTILLERY

'We once more entered the train, this time for Tullamore, where, on arrival, we were just in time to see a National Demonstration. A procession, headed by a band of music, came in sight, followed by a rickety jaunting car, drawn by a venerable horse, rather groggy on its legs … we enjoyed the fun immensely, and got mixed up with the crowd, feeling quite content for the time being to quaff Daly's Whisky, so freely offered us, and were almost induced to join their ranks.' Alfred Barnard, 1887

In 1829 Michael Molloy established a distillery on the banks of the river Clodagh, where distilling is known to have taken place since 1790. Tullamore was, and is, a thriving market town in the Irish midlands, surrounded by good barley land and with ready access both to canals and railway.

On Molloy's death in 1857, the distillery passed to his nephew, Bernard Daly, and then on to his son, Captain Bernard Daly. Bernard Junior, however, was more interested in horses than in distilling, and promoted a young engineer named Daniel Edmond Williams to the position of General Manager.

It was either a stroke of good fortune, or Daly was a good judge of character, for the enterprising Williams took the place in hand and the distillery thrived. Under Williams the distillery got electricity and telephones, and started to market 'Tullamore Dew'. The brand, a pun on his initials (DE Williams), was a huge success and the slogan 'Give every man his dew,' passed into the language.

In 1901 worldwide sales of Irish whiskey peaked at ten million cases, and two years later the Williams family gained control of the distillery. But the good times didn't last long – by the mid-1920s, Tullamore was struggling and the Williams family took the decision to stop distilling. The stills were cold for thirteen long years.

In 1947, a decade after the distillery reopened, Desmond Williams, grandson of DE Williams, took a trip to the United States. Everywhere he went, he heard the same story. Irish whiskey was too strong, too oily and too full-flavoured. He recognised that unless the distillery kept up with changing tastes, it would have to close forever.

Desmond Williams installed a patent still and set about making Ireland's first blended whiskey, but it was all too late. In 1954 the brand was sold to John Power & Son and the distillery closed, never to reopen. It would be almost another half a century before Tullamore Dew would find a secure home.

In 1994 the brand was sold to Cantrell & Cochrane, a subsidiary of Allied Domecq. 'We didn't change the whiskey in any way,' says Kevin Abrook, Tullamore Dew Marketing Manager. 'However, research showed that the packaging needed an overhaul. It looked too downmarket.'

Tullamore Dew is still made in Midleton and, under its new owners, the brand was relaunched on the international market. In countries like Germany, where it was traditionally strong, the new-look Tully very quickly became the Irish of choice.

Just as things were looking up for Tullamore Dew, Allied Domecq offloaded C&C. 'We just were not a strategic fit,' says Kevin Abrook. C&C was bought by BC Partners, a London-based group of venture capitalists. In time, they hope to float the company and get a return on their investment.

Tullamore Dew

Nose: Faint grassy slopes.

Taste: Sugar-water and malt. The latter quickly drops away as some serious grain wades in and takes over the party.

Finish: There is some vanilla from the wood, but not much from the distillate, until the grain dominates, grating the tonsils on the way down.

Comments: Tullamore was the first of the surviving distilleries of the mid-twentieth century to install a continuous still and start 'lightening' its pot still whiskeys. As such, it led the way for the rest of the industry. So I guess it is appropriate that this is the brand that has changed the most and travelled the furthest. Today Tullamore Dew is the most 'grainy' Irish you can get, and is therefore one of the hardest to drink straight. It is best served with ice and a mixer, so that the grain can cut through the bubbles without causing offence.

Tullamore Dew 12-year-old

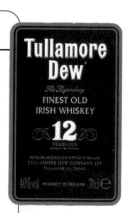

Launched to do battle with premium Scotch in the airports of the world, this whiskey is also available over the counter in Ireland.

Nose: The promise of some excellent pot still whiskey sails in on a bed of spicy fruit loaf. A hint of camphor? A simply stunning and complex aroma.

Taste: The pot still whiskey is very evident, as is some rich, gooey sherry wood. Also toasted sugar and vanilla pods.

Finish: It starts spicy, but that quickly drifts away. The sherry comes back, but the toasted sugar is now slightly burnt and bitter. One of the longest finishes I have come across.

Comments: This is not so much an extension of regular Tullamore Dew, as a throwback to the original whiskey produced by the Williams family in Tullamore. It called a halt to the tasting session, because the finish was so long I couldn't get it out of my mouth and had to bring the evening to a premature end. That night I fell asleep, my tonsils still basking in the warm afterglow of the perfect nightcap.

ANDREW A WATT & CO. LTD, DERRY

'It was almost with regret that we once more entered the train, as we realised that with the next stoppage our pleasant Irish Distillery Tour would come to an end … All too quickly we found ourselves gliding into the station, and as we neared we had a view of Derry, the ancient city.' Alfred Barnard, 1877

In 1830, wine and spirit merchant Andrew A Watt bought the Waterside Distillery, and immediately went into partnership with the nearby Abbey Street Distillery. Here he got Aeneas Coffey to personally install his new invention. It proved to be a shrewd move – before long, Abbey Street was the largest distillery on the island, capable of producing 2,000,000 gallons of whiskey a year.

By the turn of the century, Watt amalgamated his interests with those of two Belfast distilleries – Avoniel and Dunville's Irish Distillery, Ltd. The resulting company became known as the United Distillers Company Limited (UDC).

UDC very quickly became one of the largest producers of whiskey on these islands, and this brought them into direct competition with DCL. However, before William Ross and AA Watt could lock horns, a deal was done – competition was restricted, the arrangement being sealed by an exchange of shares.

Watt's business was driven by grain whiskey, sold hot from the still, and in 1915 the company's cash flow took a hammering when new legislation required a minimum maturation period of three years. This was followed by the introduction of Prohibition, which hit Watt's particularly hard. Their Tyrconnell brand had been highly successful in the US – early films of major baseball games show the Yankee Stadium ringed with hoardings for

'Old Tyrconnell'. With the enormous American market closed, it wasn't long before DCL had taken control of UDC, and by 1925 both Derry plants were shut forever.

Very soon after the closure of the distilleries, the former directors of Watt's formed a new company, Iriscot. The new firm blended warehoused Irish with imported Scotch, keeping several of the Watt's brands alive into the 1950s.

In the early 1980s, Willie McCarter bought the remaining assets of Andrew A Watt and eventually merged his interests with Cooley.

The Tyrconnell Single Malt

'As our flagship malt, this should have been branded Locke's. All those "n"s and "l"s – it's very hard to spell, and difficult for some people to pronounce!' Despite the 'n's and 'l's, John Teeling's first brand remains Cooley's best-selling malt whiskey.

Nose: Old-fashioned boiled sweets. Very juicy; alive with apples, pears and plums.

Taste: Light as a feather. There are malt and citrus, though it is not acidic, but sweet. Gentle oak when it warms.

Finish: Crisp and dry like a chablis. Very drinkable.

Comments: This is a very attractive malt. True, it is not the most complex on earth, but as it ages its character is becoming more pronounced.

Currently The Tyrconnell is matured in ex-bourbon casks, and second-fill hogsheads (slightly larger casks, with a capacity of about 250 litres). The larger casks give a slightly longer ageing time, but as this is a whiskey that matures quite quickly, you get a more delicate balance of flavour between the wood and the spirit.

The Tyrconnell Limited Edition

This unpeated malt whiskey contains some of the first distillate from the new Cooley complex. Five thousand numbered bottles were released in 1992, and there are still a few bottles available, from the museum shop in Kilbeggan and over the internet. The bottles are numbered and the label features three stars, rather than the modern five.

Nose: Intense pear drops.

Taste: A bit of warmth releases plumes of honey, melon and cereal.

Finish: Lots of gentle citrus and spicy malt. Very clean.

Comments: Cooley Distillery's double-distillation process gives its whiskeys a full flavour and body. This is particularly evident in the Limited Edition, where it is hard to believe that the malt is just three years old. This is what I call a 'light' whiskey; it is sweet and aromatic, and slips down very easily. Perfect before breakfast.

PLACES TO VISIT

The Old Bushmills Distillery, Bushmills, County Antrim
ph: (++44) 28 207 33224

The Old Bushmills Distillery is unique, as it is the only operational Irish distillery that accepts visitors. It includes a small shop, where you can purchase the excellent Distillery Reserve whiskey.

April–October
Monday–Saturday 9.30am–5.30pm
Sunday 12 noon–5.30pm
(last tour is at 4pm each day)

November–March
Monday–Friday 5 tours daily:
10.30am, 11.30am, 1.30pm, 2.30pm & 3.30pm sharp

The Old Jameson Distillery, Smithfield, Dublin 7
ph: (++353) 1 807 2355

Tours at the Old Jameson Distillery can be taken in French, German, Dutch, Italian, Spanish and English. Swedish and Japanese video presentations are also available. This is a huge operation – the complex features shops, bars and restaurants.

    The Old Jameson Distillery is open 363 days a year. Tours run from 9:30am until 5:30pm. The gift shop and the Stillroom restaurant are open from 9:30am until 5:30pm. The Irish Whiskey Corner bar is open between 5:30pm and pub closing time.

The Old Midleton Distillery, Midleton, County Cork
ph: (++353) 21 4613594

The Old Midleton Distillery is one of the most magnificent buildings ever to house a distillery. Visitors get to see how the place looked in its Victorian heyday. There is an excellent shop, featuring everything from T-shirts to whiskey, as well as a restaurant and a bar.

March–October
Tours daily (seven days) 10am–6pm.
Last tour commences at 5pm.

November–February
Three tours daily: 11:30am, 2:30pm and 4pm,
seven days a week.

Tullamore Dew Heritage Centre, Tullamore, County Offaly
ph: (++353) 506 25015

While distilling no longer takes place in Tullamore, the Tullamore Dew Heritage Centre will take you through life in a small Irish town from the early 1800s.

    The Centre is housed in a four-storey warehouse on the banks of the Grand Canal, which was built for maturing Tullamore Dew whiskey. You will also find a welcoming bar and a small shop.

May–September
9am–6pm

October–April
10am –5pm

Sundays all year
12noon–5pm

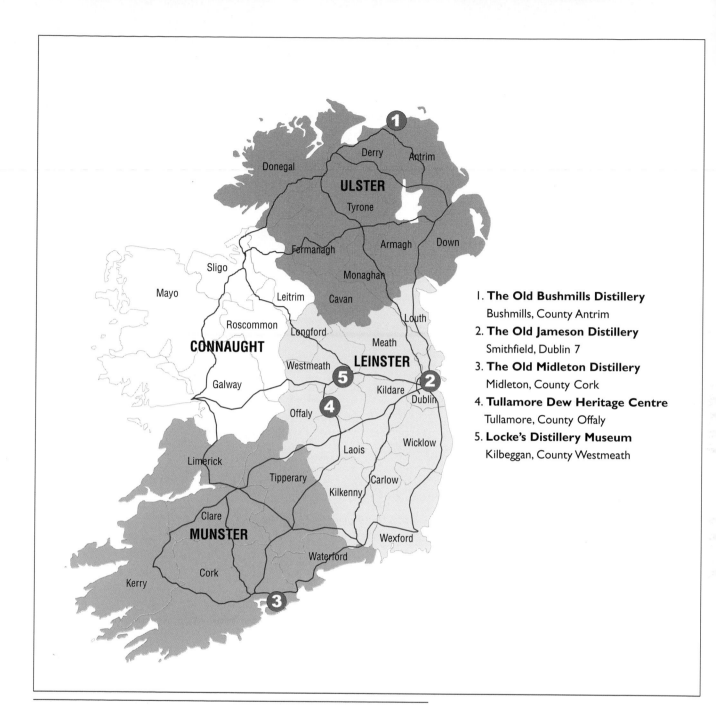

1. **The Old Bushmills Distillery**
   Bushmills, County Antrim
2. **The Old Jameson Distillery**
   Smithfield, Dublin 7
3. **The Old Midleton Distillery**
   Midleton, County Cork
4. **Tullamore Dew Heritage Centre**
   Tullamore, County Offaly
5. **Locke's Distillery Museum**
   Kilbeggan, County Westmeath

**Locke's Distillery Museum, Kilbeggan, County Westmeath
ph: (++353) 0506 32134**

Less a 'heritage centre' and more of a time warp, in these days of 'tourist experiences' this museum is a tonic. It is run by the local community, and it is the real thing. There is a small restaurant and a lovely, cosy bar where you can sample or stock up on Cooley's fine whiskeys.

April–October
9am–6pm daily

November–April
10am–4pm daily

'Whisky, drink divine!
Why should drivelers bore us
With the praise of wine
While we've thee before us?'

Joseph O'Leary, 1790–1850